PRAISE FOR CHICKEN SCRATCH

If you love chickens, or if you're a creative, you have to get this *book-book-kaka-book!* Ann Byle has taken two of her greatest loves and melded them into an entertaining and enlightening story of what makes us—and chickens—tick. Delightful!

          —ANGELA HUNT, author and chicken keeper

The benefits of raising a small flock of chickens reaches far beyond a basket of delicious, fresh eggs. Ann Byle has rounded up a diverse group of chicken keepers and creatives who share their sage perspectives on both the creative process and why they're in favor of a backyard full of friendly, fluffy feathered friends.

          —LISA STEELE, founder of Fresh Eggs Daily®,
          Coop to Kitchen® Cook, and CreateTV Host

This is the hug, the breath, and salt-of-the-earth wisdom we need right now. Escaping to Ann's house is like going to your loving grandma's and your best friend's house, at the same time. She welcomes you in with a story and a spot of insight that leave you skipping back to your own home with joyous hope.

          —REBECA SEITZ, bestselling author of The Neapolitan Series

I do not know how Ann Byle could possibly have penned a book on creativity by simply observing a flock of chickens. But this I know... the book you hold is an extraordinary achievement, combining humor, inspiration, and encouragement for the creative life. Writing with warmth, wit, and wisdom, Ann unearths the creativity hiding in a chicken coop and uses her insights to inspire and equip those on their own creative journeys. *Chicken Scratch* is, in itself, a testament to human creativity and the meaningful life lessons that can be found in our own backyard.

—GLENYS NELLIST, author of the *Love Letters from God*, *Little Mole*, and *Snuggle Time* series

Rekindle your creative passions with this charming read filled with chicken and golden nuggets. A tremendous accomplishment!

—DON PERINI, Professor of Creativity and Innovation and author of *Emerge*

Clever and quirky—much like its author—*Chicken Scratch* is a treasure. Ann has combined expert insights on the principles of creativity with practical suggestions for developing one's talents and skills, as well as tips for good business practices, and then added a generous dash of humor and storytelling. It's like the perfect serving of scrambled eggs: delicious and satisfying!

—ANN-MARGRET HOVSEPIAN, author of the *Restore My Soul* devotional coloring book

Consider this: The most successful bird species today is the domestic chicken, with a global population of 24 billion birds. Chickens rule because they shrewdly trained eight billion humans to generously provide for them, so Ann Byle has the numbers on her side when she talks chicken. Meanwhile and over on the right side of our brains, Ann brings a winsome voice, encouragement and, yes, creative flair to her effort. If the only chickens you handle are tucked between slices of a sandwich bun, prepare yourself for a more wholesome treat between the covers of *Chicken Scratch*.

—**DWIGHT BAKER**, *Baker Book House Company*

From beginning to end, *Chicken Scratch* taught me more than I came prepared to learn. From the resources, quotes, to proper caretaking of chickens and an understanding of their inquisitive and endearing nature, Ann takes you on a unique and masterfully melded journey. This city girl was immediately transported back to her younger *Charlotte's Web*-loving years and reminded that creativity lives within all of us!

—**BETH FISHER, SPEAKER**, leadership coach, and author of *Remorseless: Learning to Lose Labels, Expectations, and Assumptions—Without Losing Yourself*

Chicken Scratch will inspire you to take risks, discover connections, follow curiosity, and form a kind of nest—a nourishing space where your creative ventures have time to incubate and hatch.

—**ANN KROEKER**, writing coach, podcaster, and co-author of *On Being a Writer: 12 Simple Habits for a Writing Life That Lasts*

Chicken Scratch is one of those "pleasure to read" books that grabs your brain with fun and interesting stories, well-researched tidbits, and compassion. Creativity is a feature of being human no matter where you are, and when we're being creative we're often at our best. Ann Byle offers us wisdom, encouragement, and inspiration.

—**DAVID MORRIS,** author of *Lost Faith and Wandering Souls: A Psychology of Disillusionment, Mourning, and the Return of Hope*, Publisher and Literary Agent, Publisher of Lake Drive Books

This winsome book is for any creative who wants to spark their imaginations even more, and for those who want to tap into their creativity like never before. I loved hearing from fellow creatives— writers, poets, knitters, chefs, musicians, and Etsy artists—about their creative processes. And as I learned fascinating tidbits about these fluffed up creatures, I gleaned surprising insights and lessons from chickens themselves. The result is a deepened respect for the creative process, not to mention chickens as a species.

—**LORILEE CRAKER,** Podcaster (*Eat Like a Heroine*), editor, and author of 15 books, including *A is Adam, A is for Atticus,* and the New York Times bestseller *Through the Storm* with Lynne Spears.

Chicken people aren't going to be able to resist, and non-chicken creatives are going to be fascinated and engaged by this fun, unexpected resource helping us to persevere in our development. A great call to all creatives; entertaining while also challenging, inspirational and humorous.

—**LORI MELTON,** spiritual director and owner of The Sanctuary at Bear Creek

CHICKEN SCRATCH

CHICKEN SCRATCH

Lessons on Living Creatively from a Flock of Hens

Ann Byle

Broadleaf Books
Minneapolis

CHICKEN SCRATCH
Lessons on Living Creatively from a Flock of Hens

Cover design: Sarah Brody

Print ISBN: 978-1-5064-8413-6
eBook ISBN: 978-1-5064-8414-3
Printed in Canada

To Amy, Erica, Lorilee, Mary, Rachel, and Tiffany
You have inspired me, prodded me, made me laugh,
led me astray, and always broadened my mind and heart.
You are the best book club ever.

And to Cindy, without whose thoughtful and prodding
questions, help, and advice this book would probably
never have been written.

Contents

CONTENTS

Introduction

Early in the process of creating this book, I had lunch with esteemed publicist Robin Barnett. She has years of experience working with nonfiction authors to get the word out about their books. I expressed trepidation about whether I was expert enough to write a book about creativity. After all, there are a good number of creativity experts out there, from eminent researchers such as Mihaly Csikszentmihalyi to practitioners such as Julia Cameron.

Robin responded with this brilliant sentence: "Ann, you have to either be the expert or the person on the journey."

I'm no expert. I am a person—maybe like you—on the journey to discover what creativity means and how to live a creative life. And I have a flock of chickens. Somehow, felicitously, the two came together in the book you hold in your hands.

Let me introduce you to the flock, who I number among my mentors in creativity:

Helen, the lead hen, is large and in charge and has been since she was a chick. She's bossy and likes the best perch and treats. Sadie is the mama of the bunch, brooding once or twice a year. She is also the friendliest girl, the one who popped her head over my computer that fateful day that chickens and creativity met in a book project and wondered what was going on.

Millie and Gertie are the followers. They are happy to let Helen and Sadie take the lead, happy to putter about the yard doing important chicken stuff and laying eggs with regularity. They are dependable girls, not given to showiness or pride.

Sal is part of the flock but stands out because she isn't a buff Orpington like the other four. I feel for her because she lost her best friend, Eloise, to a dog attack. For weeks she roosted alone and mourned her BFF, but soon the other girls took her in. Now she roosts with two of the buffs. She's also more independent than the others. If anybody is going to roam the yard by herself, it's her. That's one reason Tipper the Dog loves to "play" with Sal, as they coexist in the same backyard. Sal is also the first one at the door to beg for dog food.

INTRODUCING LBC

Creatives can dream all day long about their projects yet sometimes have a hard time taking the first step. That's where the Left-Brain Chicken comes in. She's our Get Things Done chicken and takes the creative principles of each chapter and turns them into action steps. Need a process to help you move forward? She's your girl.

I suspect Millie or Gertie is our Left-Brain Chicken in the bunch. It's certainly not bossy Helen, dreamy Sadie, or loner Sal. Millie and Gertie stay in the background, analyzing the best way to get across the yard, find the best grubs, and avoid the dog, then move out and put their plan into action.

In real life, though, the Left-Brain Chicken in the larger coop is my daughter Bree, who has inherited her mother's right-brain tendencies and her father's left-brain, science-guy abilities. She created the most amazing notebook to catalog and document my prebook-launch social media activities and website. The notebook has pages to list my content goals, core topic ideas, blog content planning, and individual blog post planning pages. She included a brand sheet, a password page, and monthly and quarterly planning sections. The task was too big for me, too diffuse, too many details. But Left-Brain Chicken Daughter broke it all down into small steps that this nondigital native can understand and actually do, plus filled the notebook with inspiration: pictures of chickens. Pretty sure she could make a boatload of money selling this book launch planner thing to other right-brainers.

There are a lot of quotes, tips, examples, missteps, and plans throughout the book, but each chapter in *Chicken Scratch* brings it all together in a Left-Brain Chicken section that offers steps to put the principles into action. This is get-dirty-type of stuff to move you forward with your creative dreams. Chapters also include Broody Thoughts, questions to get you thinking about your dreams and goals as a creative, as well as your hang-ups and struggles as a human.

Throughout the book are also brief accounts of five creative ventures I stuck my beak in during the writing of this book. Frankly, I was a little scared but jumped in anyway. There is learning to draw a chicken with an accomplished children's book illustrator; learning to decorate a cake, knit, picking up the ukulele to play two songs, and papercrafting. Each activity taught me something about creativity, process, and my own fear, along with being totally fun! You'll also find three chicken folktales scattered throughout to broaden your horizons and offer up new chicken flavors.

My dream for *Chicken Scratch* is that it inspires you to take the next right step in your creative life, to realize your creative dreams, and to move ever forward. It could be a new casserole recipe, a gorgeous oil painting, a better way to perform a lifesaving surgery, a new piece of music, a new children's book. The world needs your creativity, needs your dreams, needs the very thing you dream of doing. Please, go forth and create—and maybe my little coop's buff Orpingtons, plus one, will inspire you as they have me.

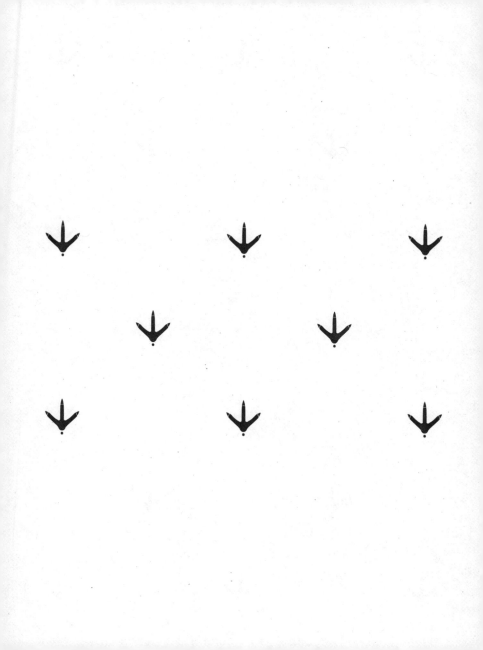

CHAPTER ONE

WELCOME TO THE CREATIVE FLOCK

THE CHICKENS

Our family's chicken story began with one wounded chicken. My son attended an environmental school where the fifty kids in sixth grade raised one hundred chickens. One day my son called to ask if we could take home a chicken that was being henpecked and in danger of dying. We had planned to purchase four chickens at the end of the school year, so were already in the process of building a coop. It wasn't done yet, but what's a mama to say when her boy calls and begs her to take a chicken?

I headed out to the school that very morning and was greeted by two smiling girls, one holding a chicken who looked quite happy in her arms. This was the endangered hen, but she looked fine to me, and I said as much to the girls.

"Oh, no," they said. "Look!" As they turned her around, I saw the wounds.

The poor little hen had been henpecked nearly to death. Her vent (that's *butt* to nonchicken folks) was a bloody mess. Once her sisters

1

started in on her, they wouldn't stop. Chickens can be serious bullies, and henpecking is a real thing. They find the weakest one and bully, bully, bully.

"DON'T COUNT YOUR CHICKENS BEFORE THEY ARE HATCHED."

—AESOP

We loaded her into the cat carrier I had in the back seat and off we went, me wondering what the cluck I'd gotten myself into and she most likely scared and relieved at the same time.

By the time my son got home from school, the chicken was pecking around the pen that still needed a roof. By bedtime she was missing.

The hen had disappeared. We scoured the many nooks and crannies in our big, fenced yard, searching in brush piles, tallgrass, the woodpile, and the shed. No chicken. We finally surmised that a hawk, smelling the blood, had flown down and grabbed her. We went to bed sad, my son probably shedding a few tears. The next morning he went off to school, having to report that on Day 1, we lost the chicken.

I stared out the deck door glumly and wondered how we could lose a chicken. And saw something move. Silhouetted against the April-gray brush pile proudly stood the chicken. I may have squawked and hopped, in part because she wasn't dead at the talons of a hawk or the henpecking of her sisters and in part because I had no idea how to pick up a chicken. Now that we'd found her, what were we supposed to do with her?

Fortunately, the college-age girl I'd hired to clean once a week knew all about chickens. She marched out there, captured the wayward hen, and put her in the pen. I immediately called the school to report that the chicken had been found.

More on that hen's story later. Suffice it to say that by the time the other four chickens arrived, the coop was completed, including the roof.

Come what may, we now claimed the title of "Chicken Owner."

THE CREATIVE

Our path to becoming chicken owners wasn't smooth at the start, but we soon began to think of those hens as part of the family, like we do the dogs and cats. We love inviting the neighborhood kids to see the chickens and help gather eggs. In fact, when a new family moves into the

> **"I DON'T KNOW WHICH IS MORE DISCOURAGING, LITERATURE OR CHICKENS."**
> —E. B. WHITE

neighborhood, I bring them a half dozen eggs as a welcome gift. They seem quite delighted if a bit surprised. Yes, we are crazy chicken owners. We claim it proudly.

When I first met Ann-Margret Hovsepian, she was near the start of her writing career and barely considered her drawing as a viable career option. Now, years later, she is proudly claiming her creative life in a big new way. While she's always been what she calls a doodler, it took her upstairs tenant moving out to push her onto a new path.

Ann-Margret, who lives in Montreal, Quebec, studied chemistry in college, then spent a year in limbo thinking she needed to find a job in the sciences. A stopgap job at a small magazine publisher turned into four years and led to a freelance career as a writer and editor.

The plan worked for a good number of years, but through those years this creative woman kept drawing and dreaming about a career that included her drawing talent. Doors began to open through writing and editing connections for small illustration jobs, and she eventually contributed to several coloring books. Then her own devotional and coloring book combo *Restore My Soul* came out in 2016.

A few years into it, something unexpected set her on a new path.

"When my upstairs tenant told me in early 2021 that he was leaving, all of a sudden this door opened and blindsided me. God handed me this big gift," said Ann-Margret. She decided to turn the upstairs apartment into studio space that allowed her to spread out her art supplies and fabrics for sewing projects and separate her living and creative spaces. As someone sensitive to noise, now with no upstairs neighbor and his guitars, her quality of life improved.

Even still it had taken many years for Ann-Margret to break through personal and cultural barriers to create the life she

> "IF I HADN'T STARTED PAINTING,
> I WOULD HAVE RAISED CHICKENS."
> —GRANDMA MOSES

dreamed of. She thought she'd live with her Armenian parents until she met someone to marry; she thought she'd then move to a suburban house with a yard. She "dropped art because," as she said, "I thought it wasn't something I was supposed to do."

And yet, she kept scratching like all good chickens and creatives do, searching for that one prized morsel.

She started taking free or inexpensive online seminars and classes on how to make money with her art and how to use software other artists she knew used. She bought high-quality paper, pens, and paints. She drew and doodled and experimented. She had taken many first tiny steps so when that big door opened when her neighbor left, she was ready to leap through literally and figuratively.

Now she's content with her living space. It's big and comfortable with a nice backyard and a creative space upstairs. Plus she's just two buildings down from her elderly parents in Montreal. She's finally settling into a life she loves instead of the life she thought she should have or the life she thought would fit her needs.

"I'm not sure what I'm doing, but I'm going to do it. I may stumble around, but this is stuff I've had on the back burner but never gave myself the chance to pursue seriously," said Ann-Margret.

This illustrator is now claiming her physical space as well as claiming the title of creative artist.

Hiding in Plain Sight

Our chickens have mastered the art of hiding from the dog. Tipper—the husky/hound, blue/brown-eyed hellion—likes nothing better than to "play" with a chicken. And by "play" she means trap one under her paw and pull out the tail feathers. Tipper also loves to innocently request to go outside at dusk, just when the chickens are crossing the yard to head back to the coop. She races out as they scatter, some heading back to their back corner and others heading under the deck. They squawk and holler and swear in chicken language at the wretched dog. Tipper grins and looks proud of herself.

The flock has figured out where to hide so Tipper doesn't bother them. They have a corner, behind some garden fencing, with shade and dirt for bathing where they can rest and not be harassed. To be clear, Tipper has never hurt or killed a chicken. From her earliest puppyhood, she knew that chickens were not for playing with or chasing. "No, no chickens" was one of the first phrases she learned.

> **"A PEN IS TO ME AS A BEAK IS TO A HEN."**
> —J. R. R. TOLKIEN

While the chickens are often out and about in the yard, they also hide when they feel threatened or annoyed or just want to rest.

Many creatives are notorious for hiding as well. Even in a long writing career, I heard myself say, "I just write newspaper articles" and "I just write magazine articles." It took a long time for me to introduce myself as a writer without the *just*. I still get a little zing of pleasure when someone asks what I do. "I'm a writer," I finally say with pride after all these years.

Another writer is Beth Fisher, who dreamed of being a writer since seventh grade. She knows it's her gifting and loves to write, but she said, "I dabble with words," when asked.

"People told me I was a good writer and I heard them and it felt good, but I didn't receive their words as truth," said the author of *Remorseless: Learning to Lose Labels, Expectations, and Assumptions—Without Losing Yourself* (Brookstone Publishing, 2020) and its accompanying workbook.

This talented speaker, leader, entrepreneur, podcaster, and writer still has trouble naming herself as a writer. The culprit? Comparison, she said. What if what she writes doesn't compare well to other writers? What if her book doesn't succeed?

"What if I mess up the writing gig? What do I do then?" she asks.

Lorilee Craker remembers the exact moment she knew she'd become a writer. She worked on the student newspaper with an advisor who went on to teach at the Medill School of Journalism at Northwestern University.

As a class they met and later walked home from Oprah's restaurant in downtown Chicago when advisor Cal Haines turned to her and said, "Lorilee, you can make a living as a writer."

"That moment was electrifying and set me on the path to writing for a newspaper for seventeen years, writing fifteen books, and having a *New York Times* bestseller," said Lorilee.

Yet years later she heard the words, "You're not a real journalist" and "You're just an entertainment writer."

> **"STAY IN YOUR LANE. COMPARISON KILLS CREATIVITY AND JOY."**
> —Brené Brown

She was able to get several scoops, one of them the time Jessica Simpson had a meltdown during an opening for Rascal Flatts at a concert in Grand Rapids. Craker wrote the story for the local newspaper, a piece later picked up by *People* magazine. She also spoke with Winona Ryder one-on-one for an hour during an interview that was supposed to be monitored by a publicist because of a recent scandal regarding Ryder's husband.

"People were disparaging about the value of entertainment writing," said Lorilee. "It wasn't Watergate, but it was journalism. I'm so proud of it."

Overcoming the Roadblocks

Naming yourself as a creative is one of the first roadblocks on this journey—and one of the most important to overcome. Are some people creative and others aren't? Are actors, writers, sculptors, designers, musicians, painters, and dancers the only people allowed to be creative? The answers are resoundingly no!

Creativity experts from Mihaly Csikszentmihalyi to Dean Keith Simonton say that creativity comes in all forms and packages. Csikszentmihalyi, a Hungarian-American psychologist who named the concept of flow related to productivity, said, "Creative individuals are remarkable for their ability to adapt to almost any situation and to make do with whatever is at hand to reach their goals" in his book *Creativity: Flow and the Psychology of Discovery and Invention.*

Simonton, distinguished professor emeritus in the psychology department at UC-Davis and author of *The Genius Checklist: Nine Paradoxical Tips on How You Can Become a Creative Genius,* calls creativity a "messy business" (another reason to learn from the hens, who understand and appreciate messy). The author Sylvia Plath said, "The worst enemy to creativity is self-doubt."

Ann-Margret Hovsepian said this: "I used to think that creativity is about being artistic, but more and more I'm learning it's a way of thinking about things in different ways. It's about thinking of new ways to do things, new uses for things, and finding new ways to understand things. You could be in a creative field, but every field has opportunities to be creative."

She is absolutely right. Everyone, I've come to realize, is creative in their own way. A former neighbor made the most stunning Halloween costumes possible. Need an octopus costume? She's your girl. Lobster? Cowboy and horse? Yup. We added a second story to our house, so plumbers and HVAC people were involved. These guys, who looked pretty rough and tumble, were creative problem solvers like few others as they wrangled pipes and air ducts and other strange stuff to make our house work and be up to code.

Remember that television show *House*? Dr. Gregory House used creative problem-solving skills to diagnose the most difficult medical mysteries. He may have been a big jerk a lot of the time, but his creative genius was clear. I enjoy *9-1-1* and *9-1-1: Lone Star* and am always impressed by how the firefighters and paramedics rescue people from the strangest and most difficult situations. Again, creative problem-solving. OK, so maybe it's TV, but still. Somebody had to come up with the suspenseful challenge of those situations.

Creativity comes into play in just about any field. Looking at situations in new ways, finding new uses for old things (thanks, Pinterest), combining disparate ideas or ingredients or even colors in new ways—all are creative endeavors.

Understanding that you are innately creative and taking that title into your heart is one of the most important steps on the creative journey. Name it, claim it, squawk it from the rooftops, cluck it to the masses. You are creative!

"YOU DON'T HAVE TO DO WHAT EVERYONE ELSE IS DOING."
—OPRAH WINFREY

CLUCKS FROM THE LEFT-BRAIN CHICKEN

Hello there! I'm the left-brain process chicken in this flock of right-brain creative hens. I'll add kernels of practical wisdom in each chapter to give you actionable steps to take on your creative journey. Chapter 1 taught us that owning your creativity is the Big First Step in becoming a more creative person. So, here are a couple of ways to cultivate creative ownership in your life.

1. Pick up a journal—I know you have at least eight blank ones—and find a quiet place to think. Write ten creative things you have done in the past month. Reread the chapter to broaden your idea of creativity. Continue adding in the coming weeks and watch your list of creative abilities grow!

2. Every time you brush your teeth, look at yourself in the mirror and say, "I am a creative person." Declare it proudly! If it's too scary to say at first, you may do it while brushing so the words are muffled (but be aware of spit).

3. Tell a stranger you are a _____ (fill in creative pursuit here). The grocery clerk, your mailperson, or the barista at the coffee shop. If you are a master conversationalist, drop it in casually. If you are an awkward introvert, blurt it out and quickly walk away. Bask in the knowledge that another person believes you are a _____ (writer, artist, photographer, etc.). If they believe it, so can you.

BROODY THOUGHTS

When it comes to chickens, "broodiness" is defined as a hen wishing or inclined to incubate eggs or an inclination to hatch chicks. Our girl Sadie is broody once or twice a year, though she has no chicks to hatch. She'll sit on a nest for days, looking like she is contemplating the meaning of life. Then one day she gets up and heads to the yard, or we put her into the yard and shut the coop door so she can't sneak back in and settle down. After a couple of days of this, she's back to doing her usual hen thing.

While "broody" can have a gloomy tinge to its meaning, in this book's context, Broody Thoughts points to questions or prompts that can get you moving in a new direction, thinking in creative ways, reframing past events, or finding inspiration in people, tasks, or events.

- Ask yourself, To whom am I comparing myself? Why am I burying my creativity?

- Describe three ways or areas in which you see yourself as creative.

- Describe a childhood memory or family story that showcases your creativity; you might start with, I used creative problem-solving when I . . .

- Name six people from disparate fields who use creativity in their jobs or hobbies, and name the ways their creativity is inspiring.

THE STORYTELLING CHICKEN: 'HOW THE CHICKEN AND THE ROOSTER BECAME FRIENDS' AN AFRICAN FOLKTALE RETOLD

There once was a haughty Rooster, the sworn enemy of the village boys. One day Rooster was sitting atop a banana stalk when he spied some tempting red berries in a patch of brambles. "I want those berries," said the haughty Rooster, and down he dove into the brambles to grab them. But the brambles were really a snare made by the village boys.

Rooster screamed and hollered and tried to free himself. As it happened, Hen came along in search of food for her brood of chicks. She saw the trapped Rooster and felt compassion and pity for him. She jumped on top of the snare, her weight tearing away the trap. Rooster was free!

Not long after that, Hen was busy looking for worms for her chicks when a hawk appeared, ready to carry off the chicks, who sat waiting by the side of the hut. Rooster saw the danger the little chicks were in and led them to safety far from the talons of the hawk. When Hen returned, Rooster told her what happened

(Continued)

and how the chicks were now safe from certain death. From that day on, the Hen and Rooster became the best of friends and continue to be friends to this day.

Retold from a version at *The African Gourmet*, "How Rooster and the Hen Became Friends," https://www.theafricangourmet.com/2017/12/ooster-and-hen-became-friends-african.html.

The following paragraph appears in *Chickens, Gin, and Maine Friendship: The Correspondence of E. B. White and Edmund Ware Smith* (Down East Books). Smith's essay, "The Outermost Henhouse," appears in the book and recounts this story:

> This year, for fun and fresh eggs, we have built— with due respect to our friend, Henry Beston— The Outermost Henhouse. No domestic egg was ever laid within thirty miles of this spot till a few days ago when, in one of the nests, appeared a fine, brown ovoid about the size of a walnut. Estimating lumber, hardware, feed, and transportation of all materiel by pontoon airplane, we figure this morning's breakfast omelet cost $167.45. It was worth every penny.

Birds of a Feather

Creativity Takes Courage: Dare to Think Differently: A Flow Book by Irene Smit and Astrid van der Hulst (Workman)

Creativity: Flow and the Psychology of Discovery and Invention by Mihaly Csikszentmihalyi (Harper Perennial)

Bird by Bird: Some Instructions on Writing and Life by Anne Lamott (Anchor)

The New Rules of the Roost: Organic Care and Feeding for the Family Flock by Robert and Hannah Litt (Timber Press)

CHAPTER TWO

CURIOSITY FEATHERS THE NEST

THE CHICKENS

This book got its start when Sadie, a buff Orpington hen, got nosy one day. I was taking advantage of a lovely Michigan spring day to work outside on the deck. There was just enough room on the high table where my computer sat to hold a hen, apparently. I looked up from the screen right into the beady eyes of Sadie, who peered over the top of my laptop.

Her head cocked and she clucked softly.

"What are you doing, Ann? What's this silver thing? What are your fingers doing? Got any food?" This is what I imagined going through her lima bean–sized brain. Probably something more like, "Food? Predator? Snacks?" We had a nice chat as she stared at me over the top of the computer, then she hopped down and headed to the yard to look for bugs.

She and her sisters continued to visit with me when I worked outside, clucking at my feet or sitting on the deck railing. One jumped on my shoulder; several wandered over my keyboard. One left a big pile of poo on the table next to my laptop. Each time I went out to write, the flock ambled over to see what was what and to see if any treats were forthcoming.

They did the same thing when I set up shop on the swing in the back corner of the yard. Curious about what was going on in their world, they'd saunter over to check things out. I count on them to come visit every time I'm outside, their soft clucking and gentle rumbles a welcome background noise. What started as two distinct things—writing and chickens—began to morph into one creative endeavor. "For clucking out loud," I thought, "I'm scratching the surface of a creative breakthrough. That's what this is, and maybe it's a book."

> **"I HAVE NO SPECIAL TALENT. I AM ONLY PASSIONATELY CURIOUS."**
> —ALBERT EINSTEIN

Chickens are curious creatures who love to explore and try new things. A tiny gap between the fence and the house? We found all of them in the front yard; they just had to see where that hole went. One time we left our back gate open, and they all ended up in the neighbor's yard. We left our sliding door open to the deck once we got a puppy and a whole new world opened up to the chickens, starting with the dog food bowl just inside the door. What a handy snack, they reasoned. Once in the door, curiosity got the better of them. We found one in the basement and, from time to time, one under the kitchen table. All five will stand at the closed glass door and peck at it—ting, ting, ting, ting—until we notice, then stare pointedly at the dog food.

Searching for Your Place

Illustrator Kenneth Kraegel's original plan was to be a rock star. He tried to learn the guitar, participating in bands and musical groups in school. "I just couldn't get the mastery I needed. I was awkward," said Kraegel, who admits to getting an inkling of his lack of talent when no one was rushing to hear him play.

As he listened on his headphones to the music he dreamed of creating, he began to draw. Bit by bit, Kraegel started exploring his artistic talent. "Drawing and painting and writing came easily to me. It is how I am wired," he said. "What I really was looking for was a creative outlet. I wanted an art form that I could participate in."

Kraegel's books, which he both writes and illustrates, are published by Candlewick, which started with Walker Books in London in 1978, expanding to Massachusetts with Candlewick and also Walker Books Australia in 1991. The company has published more than 6,000 titles, with Caldecott, Newbery Honor, and National Book Award winners among them. Kraegel's first book released in 2012, and his sixth book with Candlewick, *Mushroom Lullaby*, released in October 2022. He's under contract for several more.

My favorite is *This Is a Book of Shapes*, his first board book and my go-to for baby shower and toddler birthday gifts. I laugh every time at the absurdity of shapes and colors interspersed with animals doing goofy things. And who doesn't love a smiling emu on the cover of a children's book? My great-nephew Wesley Max (who I call Wax) laughed out loud at age two as his grandma read him the book.

Kraegel urges creatives to "go out and start trying things until you stumble into that thing you're good at. The journey of figuring out who you are as an artist is a journey of your whole self."

He says that you'll learn a lot about yourself as you explore what kind of artist—or creative—you are. You'll connect to your spirit, your intuition, your muse.

"Your art is not a separate component; it's part of your whole," said Kraegel.

He also suggests letting go when you're holding too tightly to dreams and goals. His dream was to be a best-selling author with projects lined up for years. He pushed and strived, writing stories quickly and dropping them just as quickly when the tale didn't go as planned. He finally emotionally gave up the dream, took a part-time job, and stopped striving.

"That's when everything started to flow. I had been writing too quickly; I was impatient. When I started to see a project all the way through, waited until it was fully realized, then my publisher started buying the projects," he said.

Kraegel has projects lined up for years, thanks in part to his curiosity-driven imagination, talent, patience, and persistence. Some of these qualities I see in our chickens.

They are smart, nosy birds. The Someone Project, in a white paper titled "Thinking Chickens: A Review of Cognition, Emotion, and Behavior in the Domestic Chicken," said that chickens process tactile information, have the ability to see objects close up and far away at the same time, use logical reasoning, use basic arithmetic to determine larger and smaller numbers of objects, perceive time intervals, have self-control, demonstrate self-awareness, communicate, tell coop mates apart from one another, and experience a range of emotions, including anticipation, fear, and anxiety. Chickens have distinct personalities as well, as any chicken owner knows.

The white paper describes chickens as having "a flexible, dynamic intelligence." That intelligence manifests itself in an insatiable curiosity, and occasionally plain nosiness, about the world around them—the smells, tastes, people, and experiences that make up their days. If chickens can be that curious, so can we humans!

THE CREATIVE

Curiosity killed the cat, according to the old proverb, but curiosity also fills the poet—and the sculptor, painter, architect, phlebotomist, coffee shop owner, and chocolatier. We all tap into our curiosity in some way as we go about our jobs and lives. Elizabeth Gilbert, author of the megaseller *Big Magic: Creative Living Beyond Fear*, said this: "I believe curiosity is the secret. Curiosity is the truth and the way of creative living. Curiosity is the alpha and the omega, the beginning and the end. Furthermore, curiosity is accessible to everyone" (p. 237).

Amy Nemecek, winner of the 2021 Paraclete Poetry Prize, calls curiosity the seeds of her poems. Her curiosity supplies the seeds that grow into poems like those in her winning manuscript *The Language of the Birds and Other Poems*.

"I keep a small notebook with me and write down lines that come to me, usually in snippets," she said. "I'll be walking along a trail, think of something, and write it down. A quarter mile down the trail I'll think of something else and write it in the notebook."

She also keeps a notebook beside her bed to capture fleeting thoughts that appear as she goes to sleep or wakes up. She records the thoughts "just enough to cement it in my conscious mind." Her creative process also includes a larger journal in which she records the phrases that strike her.

"I go through the snippets and say, 'That's a poem' or 'There's a poem there.' I use the longer journal to flesh out the poems and to journal my thoughts," she said.

While curiosity is the seed of Nemecek's poetry, she also has a process, a way of being that brings curiosity and creativity together.

"Walking is my daily practice. I literally write to the rhythm of my feet. I stop and pick things up; my pockets are filled with acorns, pinecones, leaves, feathers, or anything that piques

> **"THE DAY WE STOP EXPLORING IS THE DAY WE COMMIT OURSELVES TO LIVE IN A STAGNANT WORLD, DEVOID OF CURIOSITY, EMPTY OF DREAMS."**
> **—NEIL deGRASSE TYSON**

my curiosity," said Nemecek, who spent many years living in a rural environment but who now lives in an urban setting. "I have curiosity jars at home, one full of feathers and one full of rocks. I keep the acorns in a bowl because I discovered they rot if in a jar."

Linda Nemec Foster, the first poet laureate of Grand Rapids, Michigan, has a dozen books of poetry, including *The Michigan Mermaid*, a Michigan Notable Book, *Amber Necklace from Gdansk*, in the top three for the Ohio Book Award, and *The Blue Divide*, her most recent, which was nominated for a Pulitzer Prize. Every poem begins by being curious and paying attention.

"If you're curious, you have to be paying attention to what's going on around you," said Nemec Foster, a political science major back in the day. "People think you have to be really intelligent or somehow above everyone else. But anyone can be a poet if you pay attention. You'll be amazed at the curious things that feed your work."

Listening to Mussorgsky's "Pictures at an Exhibition" led to her first work, "A Modern Fairytale: The Baba Yaga Poems." Curiosity about her pregnant body led to "History of the Body," a series of poems being considered for publication all these years

> **"BEING AN OLD FARM BOY MYSELF, CHICKENS COMING HOME TO ROOST NEVER DID MAKE ME SAD; THEY'VE ALWAYS MADE ME GLAD."**
> **—MALCOLM X**

later. "Contemplating the Heavens" began with Nemec Foster's curiosity about the planets.

These two poets' endless curiosity about the world around them mirrors what Elizabeth Gilbert calls "that scavenger hunt of curiosity," the practice of following the clues of your curiosity "to amazing, unexpected places." Gilbert describes a time of waiting for an idea to clobber her over the head and, when nothing showed up, asking herself, "Is there *anything* you're interested in right now, Liz?"

She was a teeny bit interested in gardening, so she planted some things. Then she wanted to know the origins of the irises, lilacs, and tulips that surrounded her. And mosses—which is when she discovered a moss history expert lived just minutes from her grandfather's house. "Then I started to go a little crazy with it," she said in *Big Magic*. Which led to trips around the world to learn more and, eventually, her novel *The Signature of All Things*, featuring botanist Alma Whittaker.

The novel process, she said, "only worked because I said yes to every single tiny clue of curiosity that I had noticed around me."

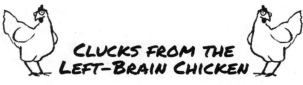

CLUCKS FROM THE LEFT-BRAIN CHICKEN

The trip into the neighbor's yard, mentioned earlier in the chapter, was a grand adventure that my sisters and I still cluck about. We saw an opportunity, presented as a hole in the fence, and investigated without fear. That is a key to intentionally pursuing curiosity: ignoring the fear that comes from encountering something new. Try these ideas:

1. Create a curiosity journal in another of the blank ones you have sitting around. Record your questions, bits of interesting conversation, dreams, and other tidbits that prompt questions. Next time you are feeling uninspired, flip through the journal!

2. Intentionally go down the YouTube rabbit hole. Go to youtube.com, search a topic you are curious about, and click on an interesting video. Then another. And another. Be brave and don't give yourself a time limit, just explore and learn.

3. Amy Nemecek keeps curiosity jars in her home for things she finds on her daily walks. Start your own curiosity jar. Fill it with found items, questions written on scraps of paper, or anything else of interest.

4. Go to the library and check out three books from sections you didn't realize were even there. Read them, or at least skim them. New ideas lead to new ideas.

Broody Thoughts

- How was my natural curiosity nurtured or disregarded or discouraged as a child?

- Write out a personal definition of curiosity.

- How have I seen curiosity play into my creative endeavors recently?

- Describe three ways you unintentionally (or intentionally) quash your curiosity.

- List at least five things you are curious about.

Birds of a Feather

Big Magic: Creative Living Beyond Fear by Elizabeth Gilbert (Riverhead Books)

A Curious Mind: The Secret to a Bigger Life by Brian Grazer and Charles Fishman (Simon & Schuster)

For Cluck's Sake: An "Egg"cellent Collection of Chicken Lore, Chicken Facts, Chicken Trivia & Chicken Love by Stacia Tolman (Andrews McMeel)

CREATIVE EGG-TIVITY #1
LEARNING TO KNIT

I first tried knitting during Camp Fire Girls, which, back in the 1960s and '70s, was dedicated to teaching girls life skills and encouraging outdoor experiences. Knitting was a life skill, apparently, but one I didn't master. The maroon scarf was full of holes where I missed stitches and either didn't know how to fix the mistakes or didn't care.

Jump ahead to 2022 and not much has changed. I still don't know how to fix my knitting mistakes, but on the up side, I really do care about doing a good job on my dishcloths. I asked Tracy Groot, novelist extraordinaire and gifted knitter, to teach me the basics of the craft. This woman knits baby outfits, slippers, socks, book bags, and gifted our friend Sharron one of the most beautiful knitted sweaters I've ever seen.

We started with a visit to Country Needleworks, a store so full of knitting supplies that I couldn't stop gaping. We selected a basic cotton yarn and bamboo circular knitting needles, then headed back to her house for the lesson. She showed me how to cast on, then the basic knitting stitch and the one-over move.

"You don't need to hold the yarn and needles so tight, Annie. It'll end up hurting your hands and arms," Tracy said. She described how her hands used to go numb when she knitted, how her elbows and shoulders began to ache. It was related to carpal tunnel syndrome but also tied directly to how tightly she was holding her body.

"Once I started to relax, the numbness went away and the soreness in my elbows began to ease," she told me.

I immediately loosened my grip on the needles and didn't knit the yarn so tight. She was right! It wasn't long, though, before I was back to holding things so tight my hand started to cramp and I had to consciously relax. I knitted maybe ten rows before heading home and knitting solo.

Stitches were missed. I goofed up, dropping stitches when counting down the second half of the dishcloth. YouTube videos were helpful when it came time to cast off and cast on for the next dishcloth because I forgot how. I ran out of yarn on the second one, necessitating an emergency call to Tracy. She explained I was knitting in the wrong section of yarn as I tried to connect the new skein. Oops. The third dishcloth was better, the fourth not so much. I sent her a pic of a glaring mistake and she told me what to do, but I couldn't quite make it work. Oh, well. I just kept knitting happily along and ignoring that teensy hole.

Turns out . . . I like knitting! Also turns out I still don't know how to fix my mistakes. Tracy said that all mistakes are fixable if addressed right away, and I believe her. But I'm afraid. Afraid that if I unravel stitches, I won't ever get them back and won't know what to do and will be left with a whole bunch of nothing. So I keep the holes.

Knitting has a lot to say about life. Tracy describes one disconsolate day of general malaise when she was working on a new project that included stitches she hadn't done before. "I took my ornery self to YouTube and looked up the short-row stitch. Two hours later I had a finished slipper on my lap, and I realized that I had a sense of joy and my spirit was revived," she said.

The next day she read in *The Once and Future King* by T. H. White this passage: "The best thing for disturbances of the spirit," said Merlin, "is to learn." Tracy agrees. By stretching herself she found new joy on a crabby day.

She also has this excellent advice: "Let the work do the work. You don't have to pull the stitch off the needle; the next stitch will do it for you." Hmmm. How many times have I strived and pushed and stressed when I didn't need to? Knitting is teaching me so much!

Recently I went back to Country Needleworks and bought yarn for more dishcloths. My plan is to work on these small things for a while to master the basics before attempting my dream: a multicolored, large, warm afghan.

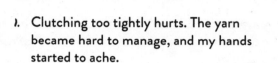

LESSONS LEARNED:

1. Clutching too tightly hurts. The yarn became hard to manage, and my hands started to ache.

2. Mistakes are inevitable. As a new knitter, missing stitches and other mishaps occur. It's part of the learning process.

3. Learn to fix mistakes. Fixing mistakes when they occur is necessary for a beautiful product.

4. Swallow the fear. I was afraid to unravel the yarn, but that is what it would take to find that missed stitch, to close that hole, to redo that edge.

5. Do it afraid. The only way to learn is to try, so next time I'm just going to unravel that yarn and figure it out. Then call Tracy or watch a YouTube video.

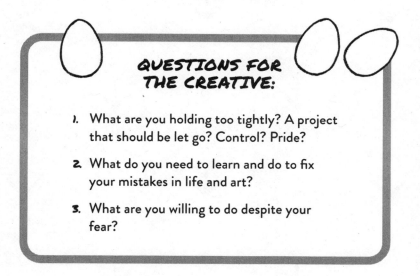

QUESTIONS FOR THE CREATIVE:

1. What are you holding too tightly? A project that should be let go? Control? Pride?

2. What do you need to learn and do to fix your mistakes in life and art?

3. What are you willing to do despite your fear?

CHAPTER THREE

MOVING FULL-FLOCK AHEAD MEANS LETTING GO

THE CHICKENS

To care for chickens is to learn to let go. They are fragile creatures despite their egg-laying heartiness. Any flock will experience loss, but the joy of having chickens outweighs the casualties that will inevitably occur. Saying goodbye to one of our chickens isn't easy. This is because some of them have met their ends in abrupt, difficult ways, a few that involved us screaming a lot and/or my husband scrambling under the deck to rescue a trapped hen or trying to free a hen from a dog's mouth.

Remember the henpecked girl we brought home from my son's school? She made good progress after spending her first night at our house outside. She ate well and her vent began to heal. Then, as all hens do, she tried to lay an egg. But her vent was so scabbed and tight that she became egg-bound. My son knew what to do: we bathed her in warm water, we massaged olive oil on her vent, we soothed a hen that was clearly in trouble. We called the vet, who recommended doing what we were doing. We called friends who had chickens.

Finally I said to Jared that we'd done all we could and we should let her rest. Then we heard the muffled *pop* that we knew meant the egg had broken inside her. That meant the end would surely come. Having no plan at this point, we went to the store to rent a movie and buy candy and think things through. The other children promised to watch over the hen, who was cloistered in a cat carrier, her head pushed into a corner and miserable.

In the fifteen minutes we were gone, my husband came home and heard the sad tale from the siblings. He gently dispatched the hen, thereby ending her agony, and buried her. It was an odd, small miracle to return and not see our hen in such pain—relief to an upset boy and frazzled mom—knowing my husband had done what any vet at that point would recommend.

Another hen simply fell off her perch dead, where we found her in the morning. Two were killed by dogs, one because she surreptitiously flew out of the coop's small yard just as my niece's Siberian husky came for a visit in our backyard. We didn't even know she could fly.

> **"AND YOU CAN TEACH CREATIVITY. OR PERHAPS I SHOULD SAY, MORE ACCURATELY, YOU CAN TEACH PEOPLE HOW TO CREATE CIRCUMSTANCES IN WHICH THEY WILL BECOME CREATIVE."**
> **—JOHN CLEESE**

Our neighbors welcomed a disabled chick into their family after an uncle, who raises chickens, brought the little gal with the oddly bent neck to their house. He thought she'd surely die if she stayed in his coop, but maybe she'd live if away from the others. She thrived! She walked, ate, and pecked around the yard looking for bugs until one day she was gone.

The kids searched everywhere in the yard. Could she have escaped? Hidden someplace they couldn't find yet? Would a neighbor find her wandering their yard?

But as many criminals do, at least on TV, the culprit returned to the scene of the crime later that day. On the lofty swing set sat a very self-satisfied hawk, remarking to himself about the circle of life and looking for another snack. The kids were devastated.

Frankly, hens have a fragility to them. They are uniquely vulnerable in the creaturely kingdom, as so many predators take interest, they aren't always wise, and their physiology lends itself to quick ends. Of the one hundred chickens my son and his classmates were to raise, only eighty survived the school year due to predators, illness, and stupidity (the first casualty flew up into the ceiling fan).

When we lose a hen, we honor her short life, remember her good eggs, and lay her gently in her backyard grave with a tear or two. Farmers may have a less emotional response to the death of a hen, but all who love and raise animals honor what each one brings to the world.

Raising chickens means letting go. Illness, disease, dumb choices, and just about every carnivore and omnivore like the taste of chicken. Letting go is hard but goes hand in hand with a fine-feathered life.

THE CREATIVE

Creatives, to build a successful creative practice, have to let go of a few things. Here's the short list—and there are many more you can likely name in your own life: perfectionism, expectations, control, self-doubt, fear, procrastination, others' opinions and definitions of success, and your own resistance to creative work.

At a recent conference I led a workshop for a room full of beginning, oh-so-eager writers of all ages.

"How many of you have to have your house perfectly clean every single day?" I asked. A fair number of hands went up.

"You'll never be a writer," I said, maybe too harshly. They looked surprised until I said, more gently, "To become a writer, there are some things you'll need to let go, like a perfectly clean house, perfectionism, and control."

A few bright faces lost their cheer; others looked like they were reconsidering mopping their floors that night. The point is that some things destroy creativity as quickly as a slap in the face or as slowly as Lake Michigan waves eroding a beach. Perfectionism is one of the meanest killers. As Hugh Prather, author of *Notes to Myself*, said, "Perfectionism is slow death."

Ever know anyone who has such high standards for their art that they never actually make any art? The sculptor who never chips away at a piece of marble? A painter who can't seem to start that portrait? A knitter so afraid of dropping a stitch that she never finishes the baby blanket for the child who is now eight years old?

Michael Hyatt, entrepreneur and author of *Your Best Year Ever: A 5-Step Plan for Achieving Your Most Important Goals* and *Platform: Get Noticed in a Noisy World*, said, "Perfectionism is the mother of procrastination." Oh yeah, baby. Not sure why we think we can create a perfect house/book/painting/business/soufflé. We aren't perfect, so why would our output be? Procrastination—we writers like to put a nice blush on it by calling it prewriting—is rooted in perfectionism.

Recently I wanted the perfect crust for the last pie of the season. I like making rhubarb pie with the crust from scratch and the rhubarb fresh from our garden—a nod to both summer and incoming autumn. But I didn't have time or energy to make and clean up the from-scratch crust. That last rhubarb sat in the refrigerator while I procrastinated until it got moldy and had to be tossed. Why didn't I use a store-bought crust and enjoy that final rhubarb of the autumn? Because I was being a dang perfectionist about pie crust!

> **"PERFECTIONISM IS A MEAN FROZEN FORM OF IDEALISM, WHILE MESSES ARE THE ARTIST'S TRUE FRIEND."**
> **—ANNE LAMOTT**

The Perfect Pie, or Not

Kate McDermott raises chickens. She is also a creative pie genius, author of *Art of the Pie: A Practical Guide to Homemade Crusts, Fillings, and Life* and *Pie Camp: The Skills You Need to Make Any Pie You Want*. These books are full of the most gorgeous photos of pie ever. Yet when we talked about all things pie, she said something that seems counterintuitive. Pie, she said, speaks into our need to let go of perfectionism and expectations.

"The creative part of making pies is that you never know how it's going to turn out. There are no failures; there are just creative outcomes," said Kate. "Pie is so forgiving. Just go into the kitchen and get your hands in the flour and the fat and see what happens."

There are basic parameters when it comes to making pie crust—flour, fat, salt, water—and boundaries when it comes to filling the crust, but within those parameters there is room for freedom. As Kate said, "If it doesn't quite turn out like you expected, it's your own expectations only. Sometimes a pie misses the mark, and sometimes it exceeds our mark."

Pie, she said, is quite forgiving as long as you follow a few teensy rules. She calls them "Kate's Rules of Pie Making and Life" in her book *Art of the Pie*. First, keep everything chilled, especially yourself. She chills it all—dough, flour, fats, pastry cloth, bowl, utensils, herself. "If you are uptight about your pie dough, fussing and fretting over every little tug and tear, you are probably expending energy you simply don't need to. Perfection is one of those things that can drive people crazy" (p. 12).

Second, set and keep boundaries. A little crust care—turning the edges under, crimping, running a cloth around to remove excess flour or fat—can prevent burning or overflow. As Kate said, "Thinking about how I handle something as simple as finishing the edges of a pie helps me pay attention to the boundaries of my own life" (p. 15).

Boundaries? What! Say no? Take time away? Not come to everyone's rescue? Not compulsively clean? Make space to create in the all-powerful schedule? Yes, in pie making and life. Live creatively by saying no and by accepting boundaries as helpful for creative work. More on this later.

Finally, Kate's third rule is to vent (not necessarily a reference to a hen vent, but who knows). As all pie makers know, cutting a few little vents in the top crust prevents steam from building up and exploding your pie. Nobody wants an exploding pie, especially those of us who have never cleaned an oven. And nobody wants you to explode either. Letting out a little steam—through a long walk, exercise routine, therapy, talking to good friends—is a great form of self-care that can prevent explosions.

"Had I realized that it is okay to vent, if done in an appropriate and constructive manner, I might have saved myself a lot of pain," she said in *Art of the Pie*.

Venting pie, venting our emotions, chicken vents. I'll let you figure out the metaphor.

Kate McDermott, in our conversation, calls pie making a "creative practice of heart and hands. Each pie is more than a recipe and words on a page. Pie is a carrier of our collective history, of our family traditions, our hopes and fears. Pie is so much more than the ingredients."

The same goes for the ingredients of our creative lives, which are so much more than a to-do list. Expectations—our own and others'—need to be let go before the joy of creativity can bloom. Obviously, there are many reasonable expectations in life, such as personal hygiene, paying bills on time, feeding the humans and animals in your care, treating others with respect and kindness, remembering your parents' and siblings' birthdays. There are also a lot of unreasonable expectations set by yourself and others: being at your friends' and family's beck and call every single minute; serving on every school or church committee; a perfect and perfectly clean house every day; choosing a career your parents want instead of what you want.

Balance is vital when it comes to expectations for your creative life. Too-high expectations can hamper your efforts (and mental health) because you think you'll never measure up. Too-low expectations and you might never push yourself. Either way, you're doing a whole lot of nothing. Author, blogger, and "The Single Woman" social media movement creator Mandy Hale called us all out when she said, "When you release expectations,

> **"YOU KNOW HOW CHICKENS ARE, IMAGINING THE WORLD COMING TO AN END ONE MOMENT, THEN PECKING CORN THE NEXT."**
> **—LLOYD ALEXANDER**

you are free to enjoy things for what they are instead of what you think they should be."

Creatives—and those seeking to live a creative life—are called on to let go of those things that sabotage a creative life. Among them are perfectionism, expectations, procrastination, and fear. When these are replaced by creativity, joy, and fulfilling work, among so many other good things, we thrive.

Chickens' human flocks know about letting go. We've learned lessons from our hens. Chickens are remarkably fragile, for all their strength, and become targets for all manner of foes. Our yard now has a small burial ground for the chickens we've lost. And to enjoy the chickens and their beautiful brown eggs is to also feel their loss.

Everyone who raises chickens has a different relationship with the creatures in the coop. We love our backyard chickens as an extension of our family. We name them, celebrate them, rejoice in their eggs, and mourn losing them. Others, like piemaker Kate, have a more traditional farming approach. She doesn't name her chickens anything but "livestock." After getting them as chicks and harvesting eggs until they lay no more, in their later years, Kate's chickens end up in her freezer or a chicken potpie. No-egg chickens for potpie with homemade crust—she let go of the former to create the latter.

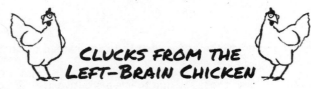

Clucks from the Left-Brain Chicken

My eggs aren't always perfect. Sometimes they look weird or are an odd color. But you know what? I still lay one every day, because that's part of being a chicken. If you want to pursue creativity, you need to create. Create something every day, even if it looks weird and has an odd color.

1. Do you have an idea you have been carrying around for many months? Years? Start working on it today— or let it go. Midnight tonight is your deadline.

2. If there is a child in your life, spend time coloring a picture with them. Watch them create, and emulate. They don't fear a blank page; they relish it and find joy scribbling "imperfect" and fun shapes.

3. Look at your schedule and find one thing you can let go of in the coming week. Spend that time working on a creative project instead.

Broody Thoughts

- How have procrastination, perfectionism, and expectations—mine and others'—hurt my creative life?

- Where and how do I need to set boundaries to help nurture my creative life?

- Which aspect of Kate McDermott's pie advice do I need to learn from most?

- What are some ways I can practice physical, emotional, mental, and spiritual self-care?

- Make a pie this week and ponder your creative life—with all its ingredients, boundaries, and unexpected results—while doing so.

Birds of a Feather

Your Best Year Ever: A 5-Step Plan for Achieving Your Most Important Goals by Michael Hyatt (Baker Books)

Art of the Pie: A Practical Guide to Homemade Crusts, Fillings, and Life by Kate McDermott (Countryman)

Creativity: A Short and Cheerful Guide by John Cleese (Crown)

CHAPTER FOUR

SAYING NO TO NEGATIVE SELF-CLUCKS

THE CHICKENS

Our little flock chitchats all the time. They murmur quietly as they settle in for the night, cluck contentedly as they roam the yard. They report intruders and I'm pretty sure offer up a wide range of bad words when our dog decides to "play" with one of them.

I have a granddog, Momo, who comes over for day care once or twice a week. He would love to "play" with the chickens too. Their voices let me know they are discontent with hanging out in their little fenced yard instead of the larger yard. When I tell them it's in the interest of not being murdered by Momo, they're still annoyed.

The girls, especially Sadie, seem to respond when I try to speak hen, clucking and cooing quietly to them. I feel like they're telling me, in what chicken language I understand, that I'm one of the flock. Me and the girls have long discussions, reminding me of talking with young children who have lots of language but have not yet formed a lot of actual words. When our friend Ruthie, not quite two years old, comes for a visit and we have elaborate conversations about important stuff, I barely catch just a few words like "book," "doggie," and "Dada." It's kind of like talking with the chickens: all of us saying a lot of things the other gets only a portion of, but still having a grand time and, as best we can, communicating.

One *Scientific American* article, titled "Fowl Language: AI Decodes the Nuances of Chicken 'Speech,'" calls chickens "loquacious." In the article, a chicken farmer named Kevin Mitchell described patterns of "speech" in his many chickens, including their "robust concert of clucks, chortles and caws" in the mornings. One morning he entered the chicken house and didn't hear much of anything. He discovered that an automated light system hadn't turned the lights off the night before, which kept the chickens up all night. They were sleepy and lethargic the next morning. No chatterboxes that day, which isn't surprising for anyone who can't function in the morning without a cup of coffee or three.

Melissa Caughey, author of *How to Speak Chicken: Why Your Chickens Do What They Do & Say What They Say*, knows

> ## "STUDYING COWS, PIGS AND CHICKENS CAN HELP AN ACTOR DEVELOP HIS CHARACTER. THERE ARE A LOT OF THINGS I LEARNED FROM ANIMALS. ONE WAS THAT THEY COULDN'T HISS OR BOO ME."
> **—JAMES DEAN**

her chickens' vernacular. This flock owner sat quietly with her chickens to learn their language. She began to hear their sounds for greeting, warning, crowing, danger alerts, settling disputes, announcing an egg on the way, announcing an egg has been laid, and saying good night. She learned so many different sounds of chicken-speak that she wrote a book on the topic, which is quite popular among chicken folk.

Artist and writer Angela Hunt is another proud chicken mama. At a conference several years ago, I asked her about her chickens. She immediately took me to a quiet room, hooked up her computer, and showed me her chicken cam. We watched her happy flock putter about doing all the important things chicken do in a day. It was fascinating.

Hunt, who is an award-winning author of fiction and nonfiction, also writes books for young readers, including *The Chicken Who Loved Books*. In this book, Little Red and her six fellow hens love when Henry

> *"I HAVE A FARM AND I LOVE IT THERE. THERE'S REALLY NOTHING TO DO, BUT EVEN WATCHING THE CHICKENS, IT'S FUN."*
> —SALMA HAYEK

reads to them during his visits to the coop. But one day he brings a handheld electronic game instead and ignores the chickens. Little Red tries everything to get Henry's attention, but nothing works. At wit's end, she starts cackling "Book-Book-Kaka-Book" at the top of her lungs until Henry finally notices.

"You want books?" Henry asks. The chickens flap and cackle.

The book concludes, "After that, Henry put his little toy away when he went out to visit Little Red and her friends in the chicken coop. And he always remembered to take lots of books."

Angie is another believer in chickens communicating—something she makes clear in *The Chicken Who Loved Books*. And it is a belief she lives out daily as she visits her hens.

"When I step out every morning, I call, 'Hello, girls,' and they come running. I used to think they'd do that with anyone, but lately I've had some strangers approach and found that they only come running with me," said Angie, who expanded her creative life in 2012 by taking up photography, and then again in 2020 by developing her painting. And you can bet that the chickens feature in both creative ventures. "I understand their sounds. There's the low rumble that's sort of 'I'm just being with you,' there's the alarm cry, which I can hear from yards away, and the satisfied cluck from laying an egg. Chickens are precious."

Angie Hunt has always loved chickens, but until a few years ago didn't live in a place that allowed them. But once she was able, "I started with four, all of different breeds, then got three more, then three more. You know how chicken math works: 1 + 1 = a dozen," she said, laughing.

"DOH-DOH-DOH. THIS SOFT, AIRY-SOUNDING GOOD-NIGHT MURMUR [CHICKENS MAKE] IS LIKE AN EVENING ROLL CALL THAT MEANS, 'YES, I'M HERE AND I AM OKAY.'"
—MELISSA CAUGHEY

Her proudest chicken moment? When one of her chicken photographs won an award in a chicken magazine—the prize was a year's supply of chicken bedding.

As Melissa Caughey said in *How to Speak Chicken*, "Love is a universal language, and anyone who loves chickens knows that they speak it, too" (p. 142).

THE CREATIVE

Creatives know a lot about self-talk, and when they dish it out, it isn't usually pretty. We don't often coo about how much the world loves our work or cluck happily about how many clients are knocking on the door and how much work we have. More often than not, what we say to ourselves borders on dysfunctional.

I know because I've caught myself saying these lines to myself:

"I'm a crap writer."
"I'm a really crappy writer."
"I'll never sell one book ever."
"Why would anyone want to read this book?"
"This article is stupid."
"I might as well go make expensive coffee drinks or fancy salads somewhere because I certainly can't write."

These are words I would never say to a friend, or an enemy for that matter. So why do I say them to myself? As many creatives know, the voices in our heads can be more damaging than the reality of the world and world's voices around us.

Lauren Aycock Anderson, a licensed therapist in Maryland, owns Counseling for Creatives, a practice that her website describes as specializing in helping creatives move past their fears, roadblocks, damaging self-talk, and self-sabotage and into a free and forward-thinking life as a creative person. Lauren started working with creatives because she is one herself, playing the piano and flute, singing, and dabbling in the visual arts.

"I wanted to work with creatives because I have that particular understanding that doing your art is essential to your wellbeing. I get the misunderstandings and difficulties that can come with being a creative in the world, trying to balance art and the rest of life," she said.

She talks about how negative self-talk can be based in our minds being designed to protect us from danger, to assess threats, which means that the majority of our thoughts are negative. "The key is to not buy into it," Lauren said. "Understanding that our minds are simply trying to protect us can help a ton. Understanding that, we can thank our minds for doing their jobs and still move forward with our goals."

Knowing that the negative self-talk is mostly about protecting ourselves also helps us nurture aspects of self-compassion. "This helps with the pile-on feeling of 'feeling bad for feeling bad' that often happens when we view negative thoughts as a bad thing. We're not 'bad' or 'wrong' for having negative thoughts—they're completely normal," she said.

Lauren also speaks into the recurring negative thoughts "often taught to us by people in our lives and the society we live in. When we understand where they come from, we can further externalize them (make them something outside of us) and remind ourselves that the story we're telling ourselves is not necessarily true."

She recommends mindfulness exercises to help detach from negative thoughts, and reframing shaming and negative thoughts like "Why did I do that?" into curious questions such as "Hm. Why did I do that?" She credits trauma and addiction expert Gabor Maté with this technique.

"Negative thoughts aren't inherently damaging, but if we buy into them, that's where we get into trouble," Lauren said.

The words we hear throughout our creative lives can be damaging. Yann Martel's *Life of Pi* was rejected by at least five publishers before Knopf Canada published it in 2001. The UK edition of the book won the Man Booker Prize for Fiction in 2002. And the classic *The Diary of Anne Frank* was found in the slush pile, having been rejected by other publishers for translation into English before Doubleday's Judith Jones pushed to have it published in the United States. John Grisham was rejected by fifteen agents and fifteen publishers before tiny Wynwood Press took a chance on *A Time to Kill*.

French art critics trashed the entire Impressionist movement. One said that "a preliminary drawing for a wallpaper pattern is more finished than this seascape" about Claude Monet's *Impression, Sunrise*. One critic had this to say about Paul

Cézanne's *Olympia*: "Mr. Cézanne merely gives the impression of being a sort of madman, painting in a state of delirium tremens." Needless to say, Impressionism outlasted a bunch of uptight art critics.

Charles Schultz—creator of Charlie Brown, Lucy, Linus, and Snoopy—never could get a comic published in his high school yearbook. He was rejected every time, not to mention that he was turned down for a job working with Walt Disney.

Angie Hunt, who has won award after award for her fiction and has sold over five million copies of her novels, children's books, and nonfiction, faced early rejection and the hard realization that she wasn't good enough . . . yet. She held onto that "yet" mindset when she later took up painting and photography. "Everything has a learning curve. But once you set your mind to learning, it can be done. You simply have to invest hours and energy and some money for instruction," she said. "I love learning new things. I don't have to think (too much!) about writing anymore because that discipline comes naturally. But I love having to think and learn in those other areas. They challenge my soul, and there's no better feeling than creating something that brings pleasure to someone else."

She has learned what strong and positive self-talk can do!

"Creatives aren't particularly special when it comes to negative self-talk, but creating means putting ourselves into an emotionally precarious place more often," said Lauren Aycock Anderson. "We're constantly taking the risk of trying to make something that looks or sounds a certain way in our heads. It can be frustrating and difficult when it doesn't turn out the way we want or we don't get the feedback we want when others experience our work."

Imagine what the world would miss if all the creatives had taken rejection into their hearts, repeating again and again that they had no creative talent or value and should just stop creating altogether. Imagine a world without the Impressionists, Snoopy, Anne Frank, Jake Brigance, or Pi Patel. Or your work. Or mine. I can't.

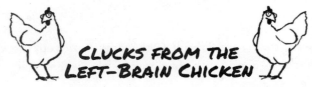

CLUCKS FROM THE LEFT-BRAIN CHICKEN

Look, I don't do negative self-talk. I'm a chicken, and as such, nearly perfect. But sometimes when I've sat near her outdoor writing station (a.k.a. deck), I have heard my human, Ann, get negative about herself while I help with writing sessions. I do my best to soothe her with clucks of reassurance. I also offer her, and other humans suffering this same affliction, these tips:

1. Volunteer. Compassion for others can bring about compassion for ourselves. Look into volunteer opportunities in your area, including a neighborhood school, homeless shelters, and nonprofits.

2. Pull out a piece of art or writing, an acceptance letter, a positive review, anything you have accomplished in the past that you are proud of. Frame it and display it as a reminder that you have done difficult and creative things in the past and can do so again now.

3. Teach someone else about a piece of your creative pursuit. Teaching helps us feel confident about our ability to do something and reminds us that we have come a long way since we began. Getting out of our own heads and focusing on helping someone else is the perfect antidote to being mired in our own doubts, and you may even come up with new and creative ideas in the process.

BROODY THOUGHTS

- What learning curve am I on now and how can I give myself grace as I learn?

- Write down negative thoughts, then take some time to reframe and turn them into positives. For example, "I'm a crappy writer" becomes "I'm learning the craft and taking positive steps every day."

- When was the last time you felt a sense of rejection, either from yourself or others? How did—how does—rejection feel? What emotions do you feel that might be related to childhood wounds? And how might you look at those emotions—as Lauren Ackock Anderson said—with a curiosity toward learning from them, rather than accepting them as "true?"

- Research one of the creatives described in the chapter (or any creative) and record how that person overcame rejection and followed their dream.

Birds of a Feather

How to Speak Chicken: Why Your Chickens Do What They Do & Say What They Say by Melissa Caughey (Storey)

Counseling for Creatives Blog, by Lauren Aycock Anderson: https://counselingcreatives.com/blog1

The Chicken Who Loved Books by Angela Hunt, illustrated by Marrieta Gal (Hunt Haven Press)

CREATIVE EGG-TIVITY #2
PLAYING THE UKULELE

I started playing the oboe in fifth grade. I played all the way through high school and for three semesters in college, then intermittently through the following years. The last time I played was probably 2009 in the church orchestra. I love the sound of a good oboe, which can be haunting in one song and lilting in the next.

Playing the oboe is all about embouchure—the correct position to hold the lips and muscles of the mouth to get good, in-tune sound from that tiny little double reed. It's also about diaphragm control, breathing correctly, and fiddling around with the reed, which is delicate and costs upward of ten dollars apiece to replace.

Hence learning to play the ukulele. I always wanted to play a stringed instrument where I could just breathe naturally while playing. With the ukulele, there is no breath control or embouchure, except to smile as you strum, and turning the tuners creates the pitch you need. Susie Finkbeiner—singer, pianist, guitarist, novelist, and ukulele master—brought her and her daughter's ukuleles to my house for a private lesson in my creative venture, this time into the musical realm. (Can I just say ukuleles are super cute?)

Susie, author of award-winning novels such as the 2021 release *The Nature of Small Birds*, began her musical career by playing the guitar. Her dad brought the family to Elderly Instruments in East Lansing, Michigan, where Susie, the youngest, saw ukuleles on display. She thought they were guitars, so when she asked for a guitar, her parents got her a cheap one. She realizes now that what she really meant to ask for was a ukulele. Thirty years later she told this story to her husband, and Jeff, great guy that he is, bought her a ukulele so she could play to her heart's content.

At my first ukulele lesson with her, she showed me how to tune the instrument, let me get a feel for the strings, and then showed me the three chords (G, C, D7) for Peter, Paul, and Mary's "Leaving on a Jet Plane." It took a minute to figure out how to get my fingers to work on the strings, but once I did we began to strum and sing, albeit slowly and with a lot of pauses for me to get my fingers in the right places.

"You're doing great," Susie said, always the encourager. "You can do it!"

Pretty soon we were singing and playing together, blending our ukuleles and voices and having a grand time. My daughter Bree listened in, laughing as we laughed. The dog mostly ignored us, but at least she didn't howl.

Dabbling at the ukulele got me interested in watching the electric guitar player in my church's band. During a particularly amazing riff, my mouth dropped open as I watched Zach's hand move up and down the neck and his fingers work the frets while the other hand picked the strings. He must have rubber fingers, I thought, remembering my struggle to find just three easy chords.

Zach doesn't have rubber fingers; he just loves playing the electric guitar. He started out playing the trumpet, which he played all through high school. He added the electric guitar in early high school when his younger brother started taking lessons.

"All the music I listened to then was very guitar driven—Metallica, Iron Maiden, et cetera. The guitar just clicked with me. I was putting in four to six hours of practice every day," said Zach, who is an iOS developer.

"You have to put in the time to train your hands," he said. "The beauty of the guitar is that the chords are set up in patterns, so you can build up muscle memory. It's all about repetition and time spent playing."

These days he doesn't have hours a day to play between the full-time job, the old house always needing work, and his wife and two-year-old, but he still loves to play. When he leads the band at church, he talks to his team about being authentic. "People have an inherent taste for authenticity. You have to bring you to the table," he said.

As Susie and I were ending our lesson, something clicked. When I put my whole body into the music, it started to come together. I began using my whole hand and arm, not just my fingers, when I changed chords. My fingers didn't move as easily on their own, but when I moved my hand and arm to accommodate the finger placement, playing got easier. It was another lesson to me about not holding on so tightly, instead finding freedom in using the whole of me to create music.

LESSONS LEARNED:

1. Breathing naturally while playing an instrument is cool. It showed me that living more of life and experiencing more music while breathing freely was important to me.

2. Music is fun and life giving. Susie and I had a great time—ukuleles strumming, voices blending—even if there were little gaps as my fingers tried to get to the next chord.

3. Move all of you. Just moving my fingers on the strings was hard, but playing was so much easier when I moved my whole hand and even my arm to allow my fingers to position correctly.

4. Loosen up. Let yourself move with the music and enjoy it.

5. Find joy in the small things. Attending the symphony is a great experience, but so is sitting in my living room playing the ukulele with a good friend.

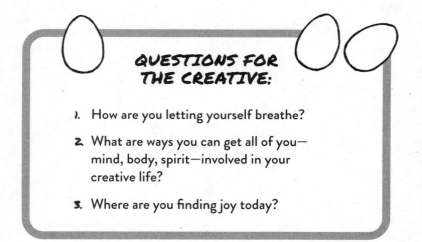

QUESTIONS FOR THE CREATIVE:

1. How are you letting yourself breathe?

2. What are ways you can get all of you—mind, body, spirit—involved in your creative life?

3. Where are you finding joy today?

CHAPTER FIVE

FOWL PLAY IS NO FUN

THE CHICKENS

Henpecking is a real thing in the chicken coop. Hens will literally peck one of their sisters to death. What starts as a fight over roosting or laying space, access to food, or establishing pecking order can become an all-out attack on a weaker hen. Feathers get pulled out; blood is drawn. Pretty soon the poor hen succumbs to blood loss or lack of food or despair.

Our first ill-fated hen came to us with a raw backside thanks to her coop-mates targeting her. Our first batch of chicks had to be separated because one was being picked on—much like the timeout when a human parent sends squabbling siblings to separate rooms. The only way to stop the henpecking is to separate the weaker hen and give her space to heal and, perhaps, gain enough strength and gumption to fight off the bullies. Or separate the bully so she can't get to her targets.

Chicks do a thing called "picking," when the little girls begin picking at the toes or feathers of other chicks. According to Jay Rossier in *Living with Chickens: Everything You Need to Know to Raise*

Your Own Backyard Flock, "the most common reasons for it are overcrowding, overheating, and insufficient air replacement . . . and once there is blood, it only gets worse" (p. 83).

Rossier recommends throwing them grass clippings as a distraction once the overcrowding, overheating, and bad air problems are solved. He also recommends a red heat lamp for the simple reason that the mean girls won't be able to see the toes of the victims because the red color disguises the toes, which they may have thought were worms originally.

"I CREATE IN ORDER TO NOT CRY."
—PAUL KLEE

Rossier also suggests letting them outside more (which doesn't work in Michigan's winter) and giving them toys such as a cabbage hanging from a string. We recently tried this in our winter coop. The girls were wary at first of the large green orb hanging from the ceiling, but three days later the cabbage had been reduced to its star-shaped stem. Over the course of the winter, they went through three cabbages. I even put a xylophone in their coop at Rossier's recommendation, but so far I haven't heard any music blaring forth. Mostly they just stare at it rather than pecking out some notes, but it at least gives them something to look at to alleviate boredom.

There are a lot of ways to alleviate henpecking in the flock, from separating out the offender to redirecting the hens' attention to other, better things. The goal is a contented flock that does the good work of being chickens thanks to each member keeping healthy and happy.

If only it were so easy for humans.

THE CREATIVE

Critics, naysayers, rampant self-doubt, and seemingly endless rejection can feel like one giant henpeck in the life of a creative. Or any human, for that matter. Judgments, assumptions, decisions based on assumptions, and misplaced expectations are all part of the henpecked mess we call life.

Beth Fisher is chief advancement officer at Mel Trotter Ministries, a faith-based mission helping those experiencing food insecurity and who are unhoused. She told me that many housed people assume that people experiencing houselessness are doing so because of laziness, addiction, or simple lack of money. Addiction, she said, is actually in the single digits as a reason for being unsheltered.

The main reason people experience houselessness is a lack of relationships, she told me. There is no support system to fall back on. "You and me, Ann, have people who love us and who we can go to if a relationship goes bad, or we don't have money for a car repair or medical expenses. Other people don't," she said.

As we talked, she mentioned people with PhDs who stayed at Mel Trotter because they didn't have a support system— relationships—to fall back on. A short while ago, my daughter asked me for $150 to tide her over until her next paycheck because she had medical expenses (trust me when I say she's very good with money and has an expensive, nasty autoimmune disease) she hadn't counted on. I was her support system, but what if she hadn't had anyone?

Those who are unhoused may either have never had relationships or didn't have healthy relationships to fall back on during tough times. With that comes the unhealthy inner and outer societal critics telling them they made a wrong decision or something about them was unworthy of societal approval or an environment with housing options.

"People outside houselessness say, 'Just make better choices.' You can't if you don't know how. We judge them based on the choices we *think* they made," Fisher said. I continue to wonder at how the average stay at Mel Trotter Ministries is just twenty-one days—as they help people get people get back on their feet with dignity and love.

Imagine the hits—the henpecks—that brought some who are unsheltered to the level of extreme survival: childhood violence, lack of educational opportunities, health problems, undiagnosed mental health issues or learning disabilities, food insecurity, sexual trauma, childhood houselessness, foster care, absence of role models, and more.

All of us have faced the henpecks in our lives as humans and creatives, and many of us also give ourselves henpecks in the form of negativity, fear-based decisions, rehashing the past, worrying about the future, worrying about others' opinions, and thinking we aren't worthy of any success we might achieve. It's important to name them, understand them: How have those henpecks wounded you?

Rejection is part of the ethos of publishing. Maybe you're a writer and you think your own work sucks; your (highly unqualified) cousin who asks to read your manuscript doesn't like it; the literary agents you approach say no; the magazines you query with your article idea decline; what feels like hundreds of publishers reject your book idea. What you experience is no, no, no, peck, peck, peck.

Fiction writer Robin W. Pearson won the Christy Award for First Novel for *A Long Time Comin'* in 2020, an honor that was indeed a long time coming. It took her three years to write the book and almost twenty years to find a publisher.

"It's easy to take on that rejection by saying I wasn't doing something right, that I'm not good enough, that writing isn't what I'm supposed to do," said Pearson, who admits to knowing nothing about chickens except how to cook them. Reflecting on her struggles, she spoke about her faith, about beginning to understand that it wasn't about something she did right or didn't do right. Ultimately, she said, "I had to not let others tell me who I am."

In 2024, Pearson's fourth novel is planned for release. And she's considering a new writing direction with a book for children. Despite the decades-long wait for publication, Pearson kept moving forward through years of parenting and homeschooling, writing, submissions to publishers—and waiting for a yes. When

> **"I DREAM OF A BETTER TOMORROW WHERE CHICKENS CAN CROSS THE ROAD AND NOT BE QUESTIONED ABOUT THEIR MOTIVES."**
> **—RALPH WALDO EMERSON**

we talked she told me about those things that fuel her creativity—writing and playing the piano—but for now, she had to go teach an algebra lesson to one of her kids.

Skillshare is an online learning platform that provides creatives a way to share their knowledge through classes that subscribers watch. Topics are literally anything, from drawing flowers to creating a social media schedule, from home styling to money management. My daughter, the Left-Brain Chicken, subscribes and has watched tutorials on linoprinting, creating e-books, learning the drawing app Procreate, building creative habits, and how to launch a creative business and find your creative style. The Skillshare blog in November 2020 addressed overcoming self-doubt with help from eight creatives.

"When we internalize that doubt and use it as a weapon against ourselves, it can become crippling," the blog said, going on to list eight ways creatives deal with self-doubt:

1. They build a support system.
2. They throw themselves into their work.
3. They stay in the moment.
4. They focus on the positive.
5. They remember what it felt like to discover their passion.
6. They don't measure their worth by anyone else's standards.
7. They turn doubt to their advantage.
8. They face their fears head-on.

"But, no matter what, they start by acknowledging their doubts and actively replacing them with activities that boost their self-confidence," according to the post.

Doubting vs. Doing

Obviously self-doubt is a big issue for creatives—well, for many people, but creatives seem to be quite good at it. Maybe because we aren't always "accomplishing things" (to echo my mother's desire to accomplish a list of things every day) like helping Third World villages access clean water, sewing our own clothes, canning fifty quarts of tomatoes, cleaning the oven, or helping end hunger in your city. If any of those are what you love and you can be creative doing those things, wonderful! More power to you.

For those who create in other ways, perhaps a hint of self-doubt can creep in. Doubt—questioning the truth of your calling and gifts or distrusting them—can be paralyzing. Learning to differentiate between doubt and reality is a first step in moving past it. Maybe you feel like you don't have the wisdom to discern between the two. Ask! Ask a friend; ask yourself what's real and what's just doubt. If you have a faith tradition, ask your spiritual center. There's a verse of scripture I return to: "If any of you lacks wisdom, you should ask God, who gives generously to all without finding fault, and it will be given to you. But when you ask, you must believe and not doubt, because the one who doubts is like a wave of the sea, blown and tossed by the wind."

If you've ever seen Lake Superior in a storm or witnessed a hurricane, you know what being "blown and tossed by the wind" looks like. But how do you move past the doubt?

Take a step. Move forward. Do it scared. Do it anyway.

As the inestimable Jen Sincero said in the megaseller *You Are a Badass*:

> You'll have to believe in things you can't see as well as some things that you have full-on proof are impossible. You're gonna have to push past your fears, fail over and over again and make a habit of doing thing you're not so comfy doing. You're going to have to let go of old, limiting beliefs and cling to your decision to create the life you desire like your life depends on it.

> Because guess what? Your life does depend on it.

> As challenging as this may sound, it's nowhere near as brutal as waking up in the middle of the night feeling like someone parked a car on your chest, crushed under the realization that your life is zooming by and you have yet to start living it in a way that has any real meaning to you. (pp. 13–14)

Seeing the Link

The website www.verywellmind.com published an article titled "The Link between Depression and Creativity," which purported to discover if there is a link between mood disorders and creative ability. The piece pointed to well-known creatives who allegedly suffered from depression and/or other mental health issues, including painter Vincent van Gogh, writer Sylvia Plath, and artist Frida Kahlo, yet the article came to an unexpected conclusion about creativity and mental health.

"Evidence does not indicate that having a mood disorder enhances an individual's artistic ability," the paper said. "Rather, the high-pressure and hectic lifestyles of many artists may lead to depressive symptoms, as tight deadlines, high expectations, fierce criticism, and intense travel are common for such individuals."

What may be the case is that creative pursuits can be a big help for people suffering mental distress. Think about art therapy, dance, Robin Pearson's playing the piano, journaling, singing at the top of your lungs in the car, puzzling, papercrafting, knitting. In fact, creative pursuits outside your usual life and work lane can be a great help in calming your mind.

Recently I interviewed trauma therapist Susan Littlejohn for a magazine article. We talked specifically about PTSD (post-traumatic stress disorder) and how trauma can isolate us, causing us to be afraid, think no one understands, withdraw. Littlejohn, in her practice, encourages patients to practice mindfulness and prescribes long walks daily, along with a host of other therapies, including finding a creative outlet. She said she recommended Johann Hari's book *Lost Connections: Why You're Depressed and How to Find Hope* for its emphasis on building connections as a way through some of these tough issues.

"YOU CAN'T USE UP CREATIVITY. THE MORE YOU USE, THE MORE YOU HAVE."

—MAYA ANGELOU

"Nothing is more isolating than trauma. Part of getting better is reconnecting to ourselves, our childhood, one another, our bodies, the world, and our creativity," Susan said.

Our creativity.

Julia Cameron, author of the beloved book on the creative process *The Artist's Way*, has also written *It's Never Too Late to Begin Again: Discovering Creativity and Meaning at Midlife and Beyond.* Here's what she said about creative work and questioning ourselves: "Every person experiences self-doubt at one time or another. In the throes of it, the prospects look dismal. We are in what feels like a drought, crawling forward, hoping for water, seeing nothing promising on the horizon. If we give in to our skepticism, we may start to convince ourselves that nothing will ever be on the horizon."

There is always something on the horizon. We can henpeck our creative lives to death with crappy and inaccurate feelings about ourselves, doubt, and fear. We can allow others to henpeck our creative lives with criticism, negativity, sneaky side comments, and sabotage. Or we can acknowledge the pain, ask the hard questions, stop the downward spiral, calm the storms within, and move forward. Every person has a different journey into and through the creative process. What does such a journey look like for you? We must stop the voices within and without and move forward in our creative lives.

As Cameron said, "The answer is always creativity" (p. xv).

CLUCKS FROM THE LEFT-BRAIN CHICKEN

I was henpecked once. Dealing with the pokes, hits, and rejection from others is no walk in the chicken run. A convenient hungry hawk dealt with my main attacker. Assuming you can't get rid of yours the same way, here is some advice from one henpecked soul to another:

1. Talk to someone in your field who is further along the creative road than you. That person has probably gone through similar setbacks and rejections and can offer an empathetic shoulder to cry on. And perhaps a "hungry hawk" of your own to help with any dispatching needs.

2. Find perspective. Received your twentieth rejection letter? Well, it wasn't your fiftieth. Your highly unqualified cousin hates your manuscript? He has read a total of three books since 1995. You haven't sold any art on Etsy for your side hustle yet? You can still put food on the table thanks to your day job.

3. Be brave and have courage. This creative world can be a daunting place, full of valleys and cliffs and unscalable mountains. But take heart. The valleys can hold marvelous waterfalls and refreshing streams, and the view from on top of the cliffs and mountains is stunning.

BROODY THOUGHTS

- What assumptions and beliefs do you have about your worth as a creative person?

- Create a movie in your imagination in which you respond in a healthy way to those who critique your work.

- How have you allowed others to henpeck you, and how have you henpecked others?

- Think about a recent experience with someone who has had so much henpecking without resources for recovery that houselessness has been their only option. Or someone you know where your assumptions and the assumptions of others simply weren't lifegiving for you or for them? What were your assumptions about this individual? How might you change those assumptions? And what could that change for you and for them?

- Research ways in which you can use your creativity outside your usual outlets. If you're a writer, maybe explore how music can offer up a different creative understanding or outlet. What appeals to you? Are you ready to give it a try?

Birds of a Feather

Living with Chickens: Everything You Need to Know to Raise Your Own Backyard Flock by Jay Rossier, photographs by Geoff Hanson (The Lyons Press)

It's Never Too Late to Begin Again: Discovering Creativity and Meaning at Midlife and Beyond and *The Artist's Way: A Spiritual Path to Higher Creativity* by Julia Cameron (TarcherPerigree)

Skillshare (www.skillshare.com)

You Are a Badass: How to Stop Doubting Your Greatness and Start Living an Awesome Life by Jen Sincero (Running Press)

CHAPTER SIX

FLYING THE COOP FOR FUN

THE CHICKENS

Our chickens are the first to check out any new activity taking place in the yard, anybody who visits, and any possible new food sources. They love marshmallows and graham crackers (thanks to unsuspecting s'more makers); dog food stolen from the dog bowl; all kinds of cereal, including Kix, Crispix, and Lucky Charms; watermelon; and corn on the cob. They will come dangerously close to my husband's axe as he chops wood. They'll rush over to check anything we toss into the coop, necks extended and eyes bright.

When Isabella Rossellini, the actress, philanthropist, and chicken owner, wrote about her chickens in *My Chickens and I*, a gifty sort of book that combines Isabella's drawings and chicken story, and color photographs by Patrice Casanova, she describes one of her chickens this way: "This one has two nicknames: Red for the color of her feathers and Amelia Earhart because she is fearlessly adventurous, just like the aviator. While the other chickens mostly stay together she wanders out on her own: I've found her on my sofa and on my desk."

Ours know every nook and cranny of our third-of-an-acre yard because they explore every inch of it. They know the cool, dark corner behind the greenhouse protected by old fencing and out-of-control bushes to hide from the dog; the mostly dirt area off the deck perfect for dust baths; the wood shed corner to sneak out an egg. The girls spend their days investigating, foraging, exploring. It's what chickens do.

> **"THE ONLY THINGS THAT SUCCEED BY SITTING ARE CHICKENS."**
> —MUSTAFA DONMEZ

Amelia Earhart and our girls exhibit the curiosity (or maybe nosiness) that chickens are known for. Hens will explore literally everything within the boundaries of where they live.

Chickens are not just curious; they absorb the world around them as learners. They can recognize their people, each other, and other animals—our girls recognize our dog, that's for sure. Pretty sure they hate her, but they also know that she's not going to kill them for sport like other dogs that occasionally visit. Play, yes. Kill, no. Still hate, yes.

The website Free from Harm posted an article titled "Chicken Behavior: An Overview of Recent Science." The author referenced a January 2013 story in *Scientific American*, titled "The Startling Intelligence of the Common Chicken," by Carolyn K. Smith, in which she describes chicken behaviors, including comparisons between themselves and others in the flock; learning from others in the group; recognizing social status; learning from flock leaders; problem-solving; relationship building; and coordinating group activities. Chickens, despite what some think, are smart creatures who become intimately acquainted with their surroundings.

I mentioned Melissa Caughey earlier, author of *How to Speak Chicken*. She describes a friend's chickens who got into her garden daily despite a high chicken-wire fence and clipping the hens' wings to prevent them from flying. The owner decided to solve this mystery and save her produce, so set out to spy on them.

"It didn't take long for one of the girls to hop up on the fence, which sagged a bit toward the ground. Then another hen hopped up, and another. When the fence was low enough from the combined weight, they could reach off-limits vegetables and plants. Problem solved!" (p. 116).

Intelligent and social, chickens love to explore and will figure out ways to get what they want within the boundaries of their world. I hesitate to tell them this, but those characteristics are remarkably similar to Tipper Two Byle, the dog they love to hate.

THE CREATIVE

Creativity doesn't exist in a vacuum. Each of us works within the margins of our art, learning the rules before bending them. Artist Pablo Picasso said, "Learn the rules like a pro, so you can break them like an artist." Variations on this from others include, "Learn the rules so you can break them" and "Learn the rules before you break them." Creative people understand that their specific endeavor has boundaries yet continue to explore every possibility within those parameters, as well as occasionally push them.

Leslie (Prevish) Rowe is owner of Prevish Marketing, a strategic marketing firm that helps for-profit and nonprofit organizations create targeted strategies to help increase awareness and market share. Before creating her own business, Leslie held corporate roles at Harley-Davidson and Trek, and now assists her clients with media relations.

Leslie has pitched to members of the media throughout her career and had some big "gets," including client Strider Bikes being featured in the *Wall Street Journal*. She also created a virtual media event for Ascension (which offers Catholic-based faith formation tools) and Father Mike Schmitz, host of The Bible in a Year podcast. The event was so successful, it yielded numerous articles featuring the organization and podcast.

Leslie knows how the media works and develops media plans specific to her clients. "Being creative is crucial to standing out from the hundreds of pitches that members of the media receive each day. First, I need to be creative in finding the right pitch (or angle) to suggest to a journalist," she said. "Then I try to find a journalist who may be interested in my pitch. I know I'll need a unique subject line, so I try to think of what may make someone open my email and consider my idea."

I first met Leslie when she contacted me in my role as a writer for *Publishers Weekly*. One look at the subject line of her email pitch—"Chickens and Louie's Lent"—was all it took. Of course, I opened her email. I couldn't help her with the children's book *Louie's Lent* but directed her to the *PW* writer who could. And naturally asked her to be part of this book that features creativity and chickens. Turns out that when she was child, Leslie had a favorite Rhode Island Red hen named Colleen that followed her around with a "curious cocking of her head when I spoke softly to her." She's been fond of chickens ever since.

As a media and marketing expert, she knows that pitches must be clear, specifically targeted, short, and appropriate for the outlet. She also knows there's an extra something needed to make that inquiry stand out, whether it's the subject line, headline, or unique hook. Leslie understands that a creative pitch, well placed and well timed, and that doesn't confuse or irritate the recipient, has a better chance of being opened, read, and acted upon. She stays creative within the boundaries of her art, and it yields fruit in the form of interviews and features.

Fuel for Creativity

Creative in another field, Michael Hyacinthe is an entrepreneur like few others. He manages two businesses: Wimage, a children's media company, and Has Heart, a nonprofit that provides creative outlets for veterans to engage with the public by telling their stories through art, design, and fashion.

"As a creative, ideas are fueled by my environment—either a lack of something or inspiration in the environment," said

> **"THE KEY TO EVERYTHING IS PATIENCE. YOU GET THE CHICKEN BY HATCHING THE EGG, NOT BY SMASHING IT."**
> **—ARNOLD H. GLASGOW**

Hyacinthe, who served in the United States Navy for eight years as a Navy SeaBee. He's the son of Haitian immigrants who was raised in the Bronx.

Has Heart's growth has been fueled in part by ArtPrize, the international art competition that takes place in Grand Rapids, Michigan. Throughout the city during ArtPrize, artworks are exhibited in public parks, museums, galleries, bars, hotels, and on bridges, drawing millions of people since its inception in 2009.

Michael saw ArtPrize as another venue for veterans to explore and share their journeys, and since 2011 Has Heart has participated in the event. But before he began, Hyacinthe researched what sort of art could be part of the competition. He then developed the plan for the Has Heart installation. Has Heart has had installations inside and outside, across the city, all featuring some kind of art created by veterans.

Through his work Has Heart has linked veterans with top-tier designers and companies. To this point, they collaborated on furniture with Steelcase and Hayworth, on coffee with Starbucks, with Design Design on greeting cards, with Wolverine World Wide on footwear. The newest Has Heart project is a coffee shop, opening on the grounds of Veterans Park in downtown Grand Rapids.

> *"I'M LIKE AN OLD HEN. I CAN'T CLUCK TOO LONG ABOUT THE EGG I'VE JUST LAID BECAUSE I'VE GOT FIVE MORE INSIDE ME PUSHING TO GET OUT."*
> —LOUIS L'AMOUR

"Many times vets have a difficult time expressing themselves or struggling with the thoughts going around in their heads," said Michael. "We're hoping creativity can channel positive expressions."

Hyacinthe also manages Wimage, a children's media company that includes *Wimee's Words*, a web-based, interactive live kids show that airs three times a week, and the Wimage app, which allows children to pair words and images to create artwork and books. Wimage started as a way to allow veterans to continue creating long after their engagement with Has Heart. His question: What if vets could type a word they were thinking, and it would become an image? It wasn't long before Hyacinthe saw the application for younger creatives as well.

Now *Wimee's Words* is well-known, airing on PBS stations in New York City, Los Angeles, and Detroit. Hyacinthe and puppeteer Kevin Kammeraad have a partnership with Kent District Library in West Michigan, have released several Wimee books, and are moving ahead getting Wimee into other markets. They recently signed an impressive book deal with a major publisher.

This entrepreneur has traveled the world, created companies, and stepped deep into his own creativity. Hyacinthe has several suggestions for exploring creativity within our environments.

1. Embrace teamwork and collaboration. Hyacinthe works with Tyler Way, a professional artist and the creative director for Has Heart. "Tyler complements

my skill set and helps me dream big," Hyacinthe said. "We've brought in creatives, designers, copywriters, T-shirt manufacturers, and more to share with them the long-term vision of the organization. They have collaboratively supported my idea to become what Has Heart is today."

2. Search out skilled help. *Wimee's Words* and the app exist thanks to editors, content writers, animators, and more. Hyacinthe, an idea person with huge creative gifts, knows how to find those with skills he doesn't have to help make his dreams a reality.

3. Be willing to pivot. At first Hyacinthe thought the Wimee app would be only for veterans, but when primary and secondary ed teachers saw the possibilities for their students as well, he pivoted to create an app for children. Creatives know how to try a different tack, experiment, and change directions when needed.

4. Be willing to fail. "Nothing comes from nothing. Nothing ever could," sang Julie Andrews and Christopher Plummer in *The Sound of Music*. *Ex nihilo nihil fit* is the Latin version. Or, more popularly for friends of chickens: If there's no chicken, there is no egg. If no egg, no chicken. Nothing creative happens if

> **"CREATIVITY IS A GIFT OF DIVINE PROPORTIONS FROM THE CREATOR."**
> **—LAURA BARTNICK**

nothing ever starts, and nothing starts if you're afraid to fail. Michael isn't afraid to fail.

5. Be willing to sacrifice. "There's a lot of sacrifice—of time, money, energy, and sanity," said Michael. "The creative life can be challenging emotionally and psychologically and the ups and downs of life impact your creative energy."

He credits his faith with helping him overcome challenges and barriers—often he is the only person of color in a given setting. Even in highly collaborative settings, in creative work, he feels the difference.

"My faith allows me, at the end of the day, to know I'm loved regardless of what others may think or say about my work," Hyacinthe said. "That foundation allows me to go out and take risks. I truly know that despite the imperfections in my personal and creative life, I am loved and that gives me the freedom to experiment."

Creatives—and chickens—explore their worlds, know their boundaries, meet the challenges, and aren't afraid to push into them. Doing so can be hard work; it can take energy and time, and efforts may fail. But not exploring? Not expanding? A life filled with regret, paralyzed by fear, and downright boring. Even my chickens can attest to the worth of exploring every inch of their world in search of treasures big and small.

CLUCKS FROM THE LEFT-BRAIN CHICKEN

We chickens know boundaries. Some keep us safe—our coop—and some limit us—the fence around the veggie garden. One is necessary for our survival and can spark creative ways of entertaining ourselves. The other hinders our ability to explore. Here are some ways to get creative in your own coop, and ways to jump the fence for an interesting snack.

1. Create something within a set of constraints. Draw using only the color red, or sketch an illustration using only circles. Redesign a room without buying anything. Build a wardrobe with only thrift-store finds. See how creative you can get.

2. Create two columns on a piece of paper. In column one, write the obstacles and boundaries you face in reaching a creative goal. In column two, write a way to overcome each of those obstacles and push every one of those boundaries. Now get busy overcoming!

3. Look up. What are the first three objects you see? Write, draw, photograph, or invent something that connects all three of those unrelated objects in a new and creative way.

Broody Thoughts

- How am I exercising my creative gifts within the boundaries of my endeavor?

- How might I push those boundaries to add creative zest to my project?

- What does "pivot" mean to you? How have you experienced a "pivot" in your creative life?

- If faith or a sense of a ground-of-all-being informs your life, how do you see that helping you move forward in a creative life, in creative ways?

- Imagine how it would feel to never explore, learn, and create. Now imagine three creative projects you would like to start, with a three-step action plan for each.

Birds of a Feather

My Chickens and I by Isabella Rossellini (Abrams Image)

Being Creative by Laura Bartnick (Capture Books)

Visit with Wimee the Robot at www.wimee.tv and Has Heart at www.hasheart.us

CREATIVE EGG-TIVITY #3
PAPERCRAFT

Denise Vredevoogd is a true creative. She's a poet, an accomplished pianist, a contemplative spirit who thinks deeply and has many creative outlets. And she owns just about everything related to papercrafting: stamps and ink, craft scissors, shape templates, stickers, decorative paper in all hues and patterns, a wide variety of card stock, tags, markers, pencils, paints. In her defense, she inherited a fair amount from a friend who passed away.

She also admits to being a bit of a pack rat when it comes to having her own supplies. "I love doing papercraft because it involves working with so much color and uses so many techniques," she said. "It's also practical. I love to send handmade cards, and I love to receive them."

One December afternoon Denise opened her home for six of us to gather around her dining room table. The table and sideboard were filled with supplies. If you can think it, we had it within our reach. Beautiful cards, postcards, gift tags, and bookmarks emerged from the chaos as we worked in our space.

The chatter was calming, advice and compliments flew, laughter rang. Yet a bit of melancholy hovered. Denise had lost her husband unexpectedly six months before; we grieved with her as we worked side by side and as she spoke about decisions she faced for next steps. Now nearly a year after his death, she determined to sell the house and is going through each room, closet, and cupboard and tossing, donating, or consigning what seemed like an endless supply of stuff.

"There is a mixture of a sense of loss and a sense of freedom," said Denise. "I don't have to look at all the stuff, move it, do anything with it, and it's not cluttering my mind anymore. But there is also the constant reminder of why I'm doing this."

She's keeping her papercraft supplies when she moves to a new place. She'll continue that creative work, just as she'll continue writing and polishing poems. Yet she admits to a bit of pensiveness: "It's a blessing and a curse to be a creative; I'm inundated with so many ideas."

She is moving forward and keeping her creativity limber.

This past Christmas, after the dining room table creative gathering, I asked for papercraft supplies and received a lovely stockpile of stamps, ink, tissue paper, and cardstock. Can't wait to get started again on this creative activity.

Papercraft, Scene 2

The scene of this second papercraft event was a little more chaotic. I invited my extended family over to make cards for my mom, who was celebrating her eighty-seventh birthday. There were nearly fifteen of us, ranging in age from ten months to, well, me. Four little girls cut, pasted, colored, and drew while the rest of us worked on our own cards or helped the littles. Someone was always holding the baby.

I brought out my supply of colorful, printed paper from when I did Creative Memories. (My daughters have two albums each, my oldest son one album, and my youngest son half of one—don't judge this busy mom!) My daughter added her supplies, and my two nieces brought things as well.

It was crazy, and totally fun, and every card created by a child had a poop sticker on it. My mom loved each one!

It was a joy to watch the little girls create. They were serious about coloring, writing a message to Grandma, sticker usage, and adding embellishments such as gems and yellow fuzzy balls. Children are serious about creativity, a trait all of us adults can embrace.

Sometime that December, I had misplaced my five plastic traveling chickens. I took these little girls places the live chickens could never go, taking pictures of them and posting on Instagram. People commented on those chickens all the time. Then they were gone. I thought I had misplaced them in the drama of tearing up the living room after my husband discovered termite damage.

On card-making day, my great-niece Xena peered into my small basket of supplies on the table and pulled out a chicken. Then another. My chickens were found! For some reason I had taken them with me to Denise's house for papercrafting, put them in the tub of supplies, and forgot about them. Thanks to choosing to engage in a creative activity together, the chickens came full circle back to me.

LESSONS LEARNED:

1. Let your creativity fly. Grab whatever you have on hand and get busy creating.

2. Don't worry about "mistakes." With papercraft, if you goof something up, you can cover it up with a sticker, stamp, or another piece of paper.

3. Bring friends. Creative undertakings are more fun with like-minded folks alongside you.

4. Acknowledge the melancholy side of creativity—so many ideas, so little time—while still finding the outlets that speak most to you.

QUESTIONS FOR THE CREATIVE:

1. What creative activity would you like to try? List three ways you could actually make that happen. Maybe it's to call a creative friend to start planning. See what you come up with.

2. How do you define "mistake"? Is it really a mistake, or simply a redirection? Remember, you can always put a glittery sticker on it.

3. Who are you surrounding yourself with? Are your friends the kind who encourage and build you up, or are they discouraging your creative process? Keep the former, dump the latter.

CHAPTER SEVEN

FEATHERING THE CREATIVE NEST

THE CHICKENS

Our chicken coop started with no roof, and well, you know how that turned out. Not long after the wayward hen was found, my husband, Ray the Science Teacher, put a roof on the small coop. He also converted several large storage cupboards in the garage into an indoor laying area complete with ramps going in from outside to two distinct indoor suites.

The two suites—basically shelves covered in straw—allowed us to separate a new batch of hens when one started henpecking the others. The offending hen then got her own ramp, laying box, and coop area until she began to behave. We can open the cupboard doors from inside the garage to gather eggs, access the tub of food, and generally assess what's going on. Unsuspecting visitors are surprised that we're storing hens, not garden tools, in those cupboards.

Since the first structure, the coop has undergone major renovations. The outdoor coop is now taller (we can almost stand up in it), been insulated against the cold, had a heat lamp and a hanging water dispenser added, perches installed, and a drop-down door added on one end that leads to a small, fenced area. All this thanks to Ray. He decided to hang the water dispenser because chickens poop in whatever ground-level water container is available. Every time. As of this moment, the hens are laying eggs under the ramp into the garage cupboards so we can't reach them from inside. Sneaky girls. And Ray also built the small, fenced area so the hens could be outside even when marauding dogs are visiting Tipper and roaming the big yard.

Our chicken coop is nothing pretty to look at. There is no gingerbread trim, shingled roof, or window molding. It's serviceable. It's dusty. It's home for Sadie, Helen, Sal, Millie, and Gertie.

Jay Rossier said in *Living with Chickens*, "Every chicken coop needs to have access to light and air, a way to keep the chickens in and the predators out, and a roof to protect the birds from inclement weather." He also said, "How you accomplish this task depends as much on your own ingenuity as on universally accepted principles of poultry housing" (pp. 22–23).

> **"CREATIVITY AND THE HEROINE'S JOURNEY ARE SO SIMILAR. THERE IS ALWAYS A POINT WHEN WE CAN'T TURN BACK BUT THE FUTURE LOOKS TOO BLEAK. THAT'S THE FINAL STEP BEFORE THE BREAKTHROUGH."**
> —JENNY WILLIAMS

"Poultry housing" can be defined quite broadly, ranging from throwing the hens in the barn and letting them roost wherever to designer coops painted to match the owner's house, from moveable coops with fenced "yards" to a coop attached to the garage like ours. As long as there is adequate light, food and water, and protection from predators, anything goes.

Susan Orlean, author of *On Animals*, ordered her Eglu chicken house online, complete with chickens. The Eglu Cube, part of the Omlet line of animal products, has several iterations, all with available wheels for portability. Plan to spend less than $1,000, which is way more than the cost of plywood, 2 x 4s, and chicken wire. There is also a chicken swing for $35, which I totally want.

That really big online store we all buy from has outdoor coops with egg boxes, caged runs, and small hutches for under $200. One, advertised

> *"THE IDEA DROPPED INTO THE SUBCONSCIOUS, LIKE A LETTER INTO A MAILBOX."*
> —AMY LOWELL

for fifteen hens and made from wood, costs a whopping $2,200. Our local Family Farm & Home offers a variety of chicken coops right alongside the metal tubs of tiny chicks each spring. If you're buying the chicks, you might as well buy the housing, too, right? On a side note, during the off season for chicks, some sly person at Family Farm & Home created an aisle endcap that featured lots of bags of charcoal, lots of lighter fluid, several small grilling appliances, and three stuffed chicken toys. I still laugh.

Even the television program *Shark Tank* dabbled in chickens, though it didn't go well for OverEZ Chicken Coops CEO Chet Beiler. Beiler, despite initially receiving a $1-million investment proposal, ended up with nothing to help him expand his DIY henhouse company into the eastern European market after the offer was rescinded. The company, which launched in 2016, had a $9-million annual revenue and $21-million lifetime revenue. That is some serious money in chicken coops! (https://www.cnbc.com/2022/01/31/why-kevin-oleary-withdrew-overez-chicken-coops-offer-on-shark-tank.html)

Daniel Silliman—a journalist, historian, and university professor—made his own moveable coop that houses four hens named Georgina, Penelope, Henrietta, and Steve McQueen. My favorite used bookstore in Michigan's Upper Peninsula has a large fenced-in area that includes pine trees and shrubs for the owner's flock of chickens. This one has a roof made of the same fencing, because the U.P. is home to more than its fair share of predators.

Chicken dwellings vary in décor, portability, and price. Yet chickens have just a few basic needs that must be met in order to survive and thrive. Meet those needs, regardless of the place they call home, and your flock will flourish.

THE CREATIVE

Creatives need adequate space to flap around just as much as chickens do. We need a place to work, dream, and create, and like chickens, that space looks different for everyone. My friend Lorilee Craker used to work in the basement next to the washer and dryer. Friend and novelist Tracy Groot set up shop at a small desk at the end of a hallway, doors to bedrooms on either side. Both now have bigger and dedicated writing rooms in their homes, but in those early days, they created where they could.

I've worked in a cold basement "office" with a dial-up modem at a desk under the basement steps with an orange clamshell Mac, in a space carved out in our bedroom and separated by file cabinets on a desktop Mac, and, finally, in a bedroom converted to my office when Kid One moved out. It's decorated with two big pieces of art my daughter made by decoupaging book pages to a canvas, then adding READ to one and WRITE to the other. Old picture frames I filled in with chicken wire and clothes-pinned mementos on; a framed quote by Mary Oliver; a giant vintage painting of downtown Grand Rapids that includes the old Grand Rapids Press building. And chickens of all sorts, including the hideous Shell Chicken brought all the way from Florida by my intern Hannah; an orange plastic chicken with metal feet found at an antique store; vintage ceramic chickens gifted by friends. I also cover my boring, huge file cabinets with magnets that say things like, "Scientific Fact: The center of the universe isn't you" and

> *"IT WOULD SEEM QUITE APPARENT THAT THERE IS NO ONE CREATIVE PROCESS, AND THERE MAY WELL BE AS MANY CREATIVE PROCESSES AS THERE ARE CREATIVE PEOPLE."*
> —H. HERBERT FOX, FROM A CRITIQUE ON CREATIVITY IN THE SCIENCES

"She wasn't always right, but she was *always* articulate" and "Well, this day was a total waste of makeup."

Using a laptop has expanded my workspace exponentially—to coffee shops, my bed, the easy chair in the living room, my parents' cabin (minus internet access), the car, and waiting rooms. Creativity blossomed in whatever space I inhabited.

Whole books are dedicated to helping creatives come up with spaces in which to work. Here are a few: *My Creative Space: How to Design Your Home to Stimulate Ideas and Spark Innovation* by Donald Rattner; *Studio: Creative Spaces for Creative People* by Sally Coulthard; and *Home Office Solutions: How to Set Up an Efficient Workspace Anywhere in Your House* by Chris Peterson.

Jenny Williams, the genius behind Carrot Top Paper Shop, an Etsy shop devoted to literary heroines, has created space to work wherever she lives. This artist/entrepreneur started Carrot Top when she was pregnant for her oldest daughter; she wanted to decorate the tiny nursery area with a nod to literary heroines, but there were no pictures she liked to be found anywhere. She pulled out her sketchbook and drew a few of these strong women and hung them on a banner in the nursery. Her friends love them and wanted their own banners.

The next step was drawing five literary heroines—Anne Shirley, Elizabeth Bennet, Scout Finch, Jane Eyre, Hermione Granger—and illustrating five quotes from each one's book, then offering them for sale on Etsy. Buyers could purchase prints individually or choose five for a banner. Sales grew 50 percent from the first year to the second, with growth every year since the business started less than ten years ago. Hermione is gone from the original list due to copyright issues, though we all know she is a true heroine. The year 2020 saw a huge growth spurt, which Jenny attributes to people sending her products to friends during the pandemic.

Now this artist, entrepreneur, and mother of three offers a wide range of products devoted to literary heroines, from bookmarks to postcards to greeting cards, mugs to stickers to coloring pages. She expanded the number of heroines—Emma Woodhouse, Cassie Logan, Karana, Mary Lennox, and more—and added authors to the list. Jane Austen, L. M. Montgomery, Zora Neale Hurston, and Louisa May Alcott are heroines too, obviously.

Jenny and her family moved to a bigger house, which meant she was able to create dedicated space to work. "It's a small corner of the house, but it's mine and I take pride in it. The natural light is important," she said.

Two work areas fill the space: one for business where her laptop sits, which faces a different direction from the pink table where she paints and packages her products for shipping. She has

> "KEEPING ANIMALS, I HAVE LEARNED, IS ALL ABOUT WATER. WHO EVEN KNEW CHICKENS DRANK WATER? I DIDN'T, BUT THEY DO, AND A LOT."
> —SUSAN ORLEAN

her paints and illustration markers there. Occasionally her young daughters join her as she sits in her sunny work space.

Not only does Jenny have physical space in which to create, she gives herself the mental space as well. She and her husband moved back to her hometown of Oklahoma City after both worked unfulfilling jobs in Washington, DC. Once she decided to start Carrot Top Paper Shop, Jenny watched YouTube videos, particularly early ones by Renae Christine, to learn more about the platform.

She took away two main things. First is to offer a cohesive product line with ten or more pieces and have a launch date. In other words, don't launch one item at a time, but wait to launch a collection. Second is to use social media as a funnel to your email list, because those email subscribers become repeat customers. Jenny sees this in action as every email newsletter results in sales.

Within these parameters, Jenny's creativity shines. "Because I release product lines, I have to sit down and brainstorm. Sometimes I don't want to, but I know I have to. It can be a tumultuous couple of weeks as I create the products, but it's a cycle within the year, so I know to expect it," she said. "If I didn't make myself sit down and go through that struggle, I might release just a few pieces a year."

Sometimes it takes some time to get to the perfect rendition of the heroine. Jenny draws and redraws and redraws again if the portrait doesn't translate well from paper to computer screen. She gives herself and her art the space to evolve.

"My style is developing and changing, which is a good thing because I don't want to be stagnant. If you're growing in your creativity, you'll get to a place where you don't love your earlier work and know you have to move forward," she said.

This busy artist and mom occasionally has time to take out her sketchbook and draw what inspires her. If there's something about the drawing she likes, it goes up on the wall. She doesn't know where the drawing might lead, but she's open to her creativity.

Daniel Silliman, the historian who built his own chicken coop, is, not surprisingly, a creative. An author and journalist, he worked a fair number of years carving out space and time for his writing. He created space in his head and his schedule to finish the book he was writing.

"That meant starting every day at the same time and—more importantly—quitting at the same time, regardless of how the writing was going. I worked from 5:00 a.m. to 1:00 p.m. If I kept going to two or three, I would inevitably make things worse, undo something good I had done, and end the day hating it all," he said. "Know when to stop. Learn to take days off. Treat the writing like a craft."

My dad, a retired college English professor, writer, and editor, was going through his files recently and found a booklet titled *You and Creativity* by Don Fabun, published in 1968, which he shared with me. Fabun was director of publications for Kaiser Aluminum & Chemical Corporation. Fabun said this about the creative act: "Thus the materials for the creative product lie all about us, equally accessible to everyone. What keeps us from being more creative is a frame of mind that persists in seeing only the commonplace in the familiar. We become frozen in the ice of our own conservatism, and the world congeals about us."

"Frozen in the ice of our own conservatism" just about says it all. I don't want to think about how many ideas I've had that have frozen solid thanks to my fear or laziness or apathy. To be honest, it took me a year and a half after the original discussion about this book to write the proposal for it. There was a lot of fear and other crummy things rattling around in my head. But once I got that mostly squared away (with a little help from a professional), I could get creativity out of my head and onto the page. I unfroze.

We can have the best physical space in the world, but our heads are where real creativity happens. It's where Jenny Williams dreams up her heroines and where Daniel Silliman uses routine to get the words on the page.

Daniel has constructed the life he dreamed of, which allows him to raise a few chickens and have the space to create books and shorter pieces for major publications. "Chickens make it feel like home for me. I always wanted to live in a room surrounded by books and have a small farm of a yard—a garden, a big wood pile, a hive of bees, and some chickens. When we bought a house in East Tennessee, we were looking for a place we could build community, steady ourselves, and stay a while."

CLUCKS FROM THE LEFT-BRAIN CHICKEN

Have you ever tried to lay an egg? It requires optimal surroundings. One summer I discovered a small space in the woodpile. It was safe, had hay on the ground, and a good view of the yard. I have never laid more perfect eggs. Our surroundings do impact what we create.

1. Think about spaces that inspire you. Create a "dream space" mood board using Pinterest, Google, or good ol' magazine cutouts.

2. Do you have a creative space already? Look around. Notice the walls, the desk area, your pen holder, the items that make you smile or frown, etc. Make note of anything you can change to make the space feel fresh and inspiring. It could be painting the walls or something simple like getting new pens.

3. If you don't have a creative space, make one. Convert a corner of the spare room or the alcove under the stairs. If you are short on space, get a rolling cart to fill with your creative space essentials. It's easy to pull out for work and pack up when finished.

Broody Thoughts

- If you could change three things in your life to free up space for creativity, what would they be? How can you start making those changes now?

- How does your current work space help or hurt your creativity? What about your emotional space? What three things can you change to open up inner and outer creative spaces?

- Ask yourself, "In what areas have I been 'frozen in the ice of my own conservatism?'" How did you break free, or how do you plan to?

- List five creative ideas you've had recently, along with what stopped you from pursuing them.

THE STORYTELLING CHICKEN: 'PRIDE AND THE ROOSTER' A CHINESE FOLKTALE RETOLD

A widow raised many hundreds of chickens each year, which she sold to support herself and her two children. Each day the chickens hunted bugs, bits of rice, and green treats in the nearby fields. The leader of the flock was called the King of the Chickens, and he was the strongest and crowed the loudest.

One day he said to his flock, "Let's go to the other side of the mountain and find rice, wheat, corn, and wild silkworms because there isn't enough food here."

"We are afraid of the foxes and eagles who will catch us," the flock cried.

"Fine," he said, "all you old hens and cowards can stay at home."

So the King of the Chickens and his secretary started off to the other side of the mountain. On the way, the secretary found a tasty beetle. The King of the Chickens snatched it away because he thought beetles belonged to kings, not secretaries. The secretary left the king on his own.

When the King of the Chickens got home at sunset, he was angry at the others for not going with

(Continued)

him. He fought one after another, pulling their feathers out, so they left too. The flock decided to hide out in the vegetable patch and not come home until the widow found them another home.

When the widow asked the king where the flock was, he said, "They are cowards and no use in the world. I hope they stay away forever."

The widow answered, "You're not the only chicken in the world. Bring my chickens back or you will see trouble." She found the chickens the next morning when she went to her vegetable patch and brought them back to the king to help them make peace.

They bowed their heads and looked happy to see him again, but he wouldn't bow to them. Instead, he flew up into a tree and sang war songs loudly and crowed about how he needed no one because he was the king.

An eagle heard him crowing, flew down and caught him with his talons and carried him away. The proud and quarrelsome king was never seen again.

Retold from a version by Mary Hayes Davis and Chow-Leung, *Chinese Fables and Folk Stories* (Woodstock, GA: American Book Company, 1908).

Birds of a Feather

The Eglu by Omlet, www.omlet.us

Carrot Top Paper Shop: https://www.etsy.com/shop/
CarrotTopPaperShop?section_id=18199213

*The Creativity Challenge: Design, Experiment, Test, Innovate,
Build, Create, Inspire, and Unleash Your Genius* by Tanner
Christensen (Adams Media)

On Animals by Susan Orlean (Avid Reader Press)

CHAPTER EIGHT

THE JOYS OF FLOCKING TOGETHER

THE CHICKENS

Chickens tend to move in a pack. Our small flock wanders around the yard, staying in the vicinity of one another. One may head back to the coop to lay her egg, but as soon as she's done (and announces it loudly), she heads back to her sisters. They amble from one corner of the yard to the other, heads down as they look for bugs, worms, or seeds.

These smart girls know that if one is separated and the wretched dog is out and about, the dog will chase the one wandering alone. She'll scuttle back to her sisters, eager for the protection of the flock. Even a stupid dog thinks twice about teasing a bunch of hens, and our dog isn't stupid.

The dynamics operating within a flock of chickens are more advanced than we humans might think. There are leaders and followers, relationships are formed within the flock, and the flock communicates among themselves. Melissa Caughey, in her *How to*

Speak Chicken, cites several studies about chickens watching television or videos and learning from what they see. One group, who watched chickens eat out of a red feed bowl, headed for the red feed bowls when offered red and yellow bowls in real life (p. 104). She describes her own chickens recognizing the treat container and jumping up and down on it when Melissa didn't get them treats soon enough.

Chickens can influence one another as well. One broody hen can encourage others to brood, or one girl interested in the dog food soon means all of the hens are rushing in to snack if we leave the door open. During the winter when our hens are confined to the coop, they start out laying their eggs in the usual spot inside the garage coop. Then one of them gets lazy and burrows under the ramp into the garage and lays there. Pretty soon all the hens are laying in that spot, inaccessible from the garage. (Thank you very much, girls, for making us dig through the snow to open the outside door—buried in snow for insulation—to get your eggs.)

> **"I NEVER EXPECTED THAT I WOULD BE FRIENDS WITH A CHICKEN, BUT THAT IS THE WONDERFUL THING ABOUT LIFE'S JOURNEY. IF YOU TAKE THE TIME TO EXPLORE SOMETHING NEW IN THIS WORLD, OFTEN THE UNEXPECTED HAPPENS."**
>
> **—MELISSA CAUGHEY, AUTHOR OF HOW TO SPEAK CHICKEN**

The book *Raising Chickens for Dummies* is excerpted on www.dummies.com, where the site offers this about flock behavior: "With chickens, it's all about family. . . . Ranking begins the moment chicks hatch or whenever chickens are put together. Hens have their own ranking system, separate from roosters. Every member of the flock soon knows its place, although some squabbling and downright battles may ensue during the ranking process."

Living in the Flock

Lacy Finn Borgo understands the goodness of a gathered flock. She lives on forty acres on the Western Slope of the Rocky Mountains, a place she refers to as a bobcat freeway. Every two years or so, she and her family get new chicks and house them in the coop made from doors and windows replaced in their home renovation. When she's agitated or stressed, she sits among her chickens to find the calm she craves.

"The soothing tones and sounds they make as they do the things they do is calming," said Lacy, who is director of Good Dirt Ministries—offering spiritual direction for adults and children. She is also a conference and retreat speaker as well as an author. Her newest book is a children's picture book titled *All Will Be Well: Learning to Trust God's Love*, the story of a grandmother's love for her granddaughter that incorporates the wisdom of mystic and theologian Julian of Norwich. Lacy also spends time talking with children who are experiencing houselessness. Solace in the chicken coop is a necessity amid what can be a demanding career and family life.

"They are living from the place of who they are in their chicken selves. There isn't striving—they are just pecking along. Chickens are centered in their chicken-ness. The dogs try to please me, the cats ignore me, and the goats are reading me and trying to break out, but the chickens are just centered on doing chicken things."

Chickens live in their chicken-ness, happy in the group and moving within it as only chickens can do—with creative exploration in mind, with a little squabbling, and in a constant search for nourishment.

A couple years ago, we added two new hens to our flock of four buff Orpingtons. The two gray girls stuck together, the best of friends beginning when they were chicks. They roosted separately from the others, content being a clique. Then Eloise was killed (it was a rough summer around here), leaving Sal on her own. At first she roosted alone and foraged on the edges of the others. But as these things go, Sal was slowly integrated into the Flock of Four, the buff Orpingtons accepting her as one of their own. She now roosts next to the others, though I expect she misses Eloise, her soul sister.

I would never presume to know what's going on in a chicken's brain, but I like to think that Sal is now best friends with Sadie, Helen, Millie, and Gertie and finds comfort from her BFFs.

What Sal and her BFFs have together—protection, company, a family—is the gift of the flock, something I continue to learn from as I try to live creatively and well. Surrounding ourselves with those who nurture and protect us can bring such joy and is one of the best ways to feather our creative nests.

THE CREATIVE

I'm a member of the Guild, a small group of writers joined at the hip in life and writing. We started gathering maybe twenty years ago after I interviewed two (now) members about their new books for the local newspaper.

"Hey, we should start a writer's group," I said separately to both of them. Lorilee Craker, who I met when we were both great with child, her No. 2 and my No. 4 and who are now twenty-one, I interviewed when her book *A Is for Adam: Biblical Baby Names* came out. And Tracy Groot and I met around the same time when her first novel, *The Brother's Keeper*, released.

> **"A LITTLE-KNOWN SIDE EFFECT OF CHICKEN KEEPING IS THAT YOU INEXPLICABLY WIND UP SPENDING A LOT OF TIME JUST SITTING IN YOUR YARD, STARING AT YOUR BIRDS. LIKE A TOTAL CREEP. YOU MAY THINK YOU WON'T, BUT TRUST ME, YOU WILL. OH, HOW YOU WILL. SO, YOU MIGHT AS WELL SIP ON A LOVELY LITTLE COCKTAIL WHILE YOU DO IT."**
> —KATE E. RICHARDS, AUTHOR OF DRINKING WITH CHICKENS: FREE-RANGE COCKTAILS FOR THE HAPPIEST HOUR

Since that time, we've gained and lost members, experienced highs and lows, started and ended a writer's conference called Breathe, cried, laughed, encouraged, nudged, cattle-prodded, spoken truth to one another, and weathered a fair number of personal storms. The last couple of years have been rough, but the five of us who remain are committed to each other in writing and friendship.

One of our key missions for creating Breathe was to encourage writers to find a group of like-minded people with whom to commiserate, dream, find help, encourage, and live the writing life. Seriously, who else can writers relate to more than other writers? Most nonwriters think we're half nuts anyway. Everyone, especially creatives, needs somebody to talk to every now and again.

Julia Cameron encourages midlife creatives to ask for help in *It's Never Too Late to Begin Again: Discovering Creativity and Meaning at Midlife and Beyond*. Her book *The Artist's Way* was

"SOMETIMES OUR DREAMS SEEM SO FAR OUT OF REACH THAT WE DISCOUNT THEM BEFORE WE BEGIN. BUT IF WE ARE WILLING TO LOOK FOR SUPPORTIVE MENTORS AND ARE ABLE TO RECOGNIZE THEM WHEN WE MEET THEM, WE WILL MOVE AHEAD. WE JUST HAVE TO FIND THE COURAGE TO SPEAK UP AND ASK FOR HELP."
—JULIA CAMERON, AUTHOR OF *IT'S NEVER TOO LATE TO BEGIN AGAIN*

groundbreaking for so many, and her book for those with a few more years of experience on them is as well. She encourages those with creative dreams to ask for help, which, to be honest, is mighty hard for folks who have been successful in their careers. "Most blocked creatives have an addiction to anxiety," she said (p. 121), anxiety about looking weak or stupid, anxiety about failing, anxiety about appearing the fool.

> **"WE NEED NEW AND UNUSUAL EXPERIENCES TO THINK DIFFERENTLY."**
> —SCOTT BARRY KAUFMAN AND CAROLYN GREGOIRE IN WIRED TO CREATE

Yet, Cameron reiterates, ask for help. She describes a retired architect who dreamed of making films and who was finally persuaded to write about his dreams in his Morning Words, a writing practice made famous by Cameron. After the architect began dreaming in his morning pages, he soon found himself at a dinner party, seated next to a filmmaker. He worked up the courage to talk with him and ended up enrolling in his new filmmaking class at the local community college, where he made his first film and was told by the teacher he was a natural. Now the retired architect is fulfilling his lifelong dream.

Surrounding ourselves with people who encourage our dreams and who can help us understand and implement them is vitally important to any creative. We all have naysayers, negative nellies, and downright jerks who are happy to tell us why we can't do something and what a crappy idea we have. Flee these folks, or at least learn to tune out their negativity (a therapist can help, as will true friends who want the best for you).

One book that might help in taking steps toward true support is the cowritten book *Wired to Create: Unraveling the Mysteries of the Creative Mind*—a lovely blend of science and the real-life experience of the authors. Carolyn Gregoire is a writer at the *Huffington Post*, where she reports on psychology and mental health, while Dr. Scott Kaufman investigates the development of imagination, creativity, and well-being, among other things, at the University of Pennsylvania. Their book, released in 2016, describes "Ten Things Highly Creative People Do Differently," and each chapter focuses on one aspect. These include:

1. Imaginative play—nurtured in childhood and continued into adulthood
2. Passion—falling in love with that creative activity
3. Daydreaming—letting the mind wander to find new ways of doing things
4. Solitude—allowing time for solitary reflection
5. Intuition—following gut feelings and inner knowings
6. Openness to experience—a desire to learn and experiment
7. Mindfulness—paying attention
8. Sensitivity—taking in the world around you, sometimes as an HSP
9. Turning adversity into advantage—rising above circumstance
10. Thinking differently—despite society's love of conformity

If you get a chance to read *Wired to Create*, please do. It's creatively written and researched, outside the box when it comes to new understandings of creativity, and full of great stories that entertain and instruct. What's not to love?

Other books, like Julia Cameron's book *The Artist's Way*, add to the ways we can nourish creative work in the companionship of the flow. She talks about artist dates, weekly events that allow creatives to explore something that interests them. Cameron encourages these dates to foster creativity, whimsy, fun, magic, and imagination. Not to mention giving yourself a break from the work of creating and the-people-you-love-at-home-who-can-be-seriously-annoying-when-you're-trying-to-create-something.

The artist date possibilities are endless: visit a museum, take a drawing class, walk along the beach, hike a woodland trail, garden, peruse a home decorating book, visit the library, attend a concert. To be honest, I'm not good at going on artist dates. We have the beautiful and world-class Frederik Meijer Gardens & Sculpture Park here in Grand Rapids, just three miles from my house, if you must know. But when was the last time I visited? Probably eight years ago. And a date to the symphony? My husband and I went to the symphony five years ago with friends, which I thought was amazing, but he hated. (Sometimes the artist date is more successful when you are with your creativity peeps.)

No art museum. No Gerald R. Ford Presidential Museum visit in recent years. We're not complete dolts, though. The Left-Brain Chicken and I went to Beyond van Gogh: The Immersive

Experience when it was here, and my husband and I go to ArtPrize, love Lake Michigan, and visit the Upper Peninsula regularly, all of which feed my creative spirit. Oddly, attending West Michigan Whitecaps baseball games (a Detroit Tigers High-A affiliate team) allows me to completely relax and thus encourage creativity. To learn more about creative pursuits, I've learned to knit and play the ukulele, enjoyed two afternoons of papercrafting, decorated a camping-themed birthday cake, and learned how to draw a chicken (see the Creative Egg-tivities throughout this book). I've learned things about myself and opened my head and heart to new experiences, all of which feed my creative heart.

Creative pursuits, while mostly done individually, aren't meant to be done in a vacuum. Creativity calls out to other voices, other mediums, other ways of doing things. It crows when it accomplishes something, clucks softly as it goes about its business, and fluffs its feathers to gather like-minded friends to its side.

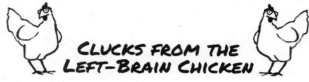

CLUCKS FROM THE LEFT-BRAIN CHICKEN

I love my flock. Despite the occasional henpecking and Helen always stealing my worms, I couldn't imagine life without them. When Ann asked me to contribute to this book, I was nervous. But my sisters cheered me on every step of the way. They protect me and challenge me. And they have brainstormed with me to offer these tips for finding a flock of your own:

1. Start a monthly creative night with friends. Pick a shared interest (like knitting) or try something new every month.

2. Check out meetup.com for opportunities to meet new people in your city. The site offers groups for hiking, drawing, cooking, and a whole lot more.

3. Look into conferences or retreats focused on your interests. Attending a conference is a commitment, but it offers learning, access to professionals, and a way to meet like-minded people. You may end up forming your flock of encouragers with people you meet.

Broody Thoughts

- What have you always wanted to do but were too afraid to try? What is holding you back?

- Write a mission and vision statement for a creative group you'd like to start, then build a list of potential members.

- Describe how you envision that creative group operating and how such a group might help you—and how you might help each other—on your creative journey.

- Describe your feelings when you tried a new creative activity—the good and not-so-good feelings. Are there insights you can take from the good to encourage you in your next steps? Or insights from the not-so-good that are lessons learned for your next creative venture?

Birds of a Feather

The Artist's Way: A Spiritual Path to Higher Creativity by Julia Cameron

Drinking with Chickens: Free-Range Cocktails for the Happiest Hour by Kate E. Richards

On Being a Writer: 12 Simple Habits for a Writing Life that Lasts by Ann Kroeker and Charity Singleton Craig

Wired to Create: Unraveling the Mysteries of the Creative Mind by Scott Barry Kaufman and Carolyn Gregoire

CREATIVE EGG-TIVITY #4
CAKE DECORATING

My children remember their birthday cakes well. Always in a 9 x 13 pan, often with strangely colored frosting, occasionally some decorations. Nothing special, except that the frosting was often made from scratch and each cake was eaten with lots of family around and accompanied by presents.

One time I took a birthday cake to a church potluck (it was my daughter's birthday) and . . . nobody took a piece. For one of my sons, I stuck a Matchbox car on as an added decoration. Whatever. Give me a break.

Their Byle cousins, however, had the most magnificent birthday cakes ever in the history of birthday cakes. A dolphin leaping over a wave; a multiturreted castle; one completely covered in candy. Whatever kind of cake they wanted, their grandma made it for them without exception. To be clear, this is not their shared Grandma Byle. She always buys a cake. Usually the expensive one.

This was their other grandma, Ruth Stephen, who used to own a bakery and who owns approximately five hundred Wilton cake pans. And serious food coloring. And myriad tips for the frosting bag. Naturally, I hire her to make the cake for every bridal and baby shower I am in charge of. Once she made a cake in the shape of a onesie, another time a hedgehog. Every cake was perfect and elicited oohs and ahhs from guests. Numerous pictures were taken.

After the potluck incident, I've grown a teeny bit insecure about my cakes, which you may have noticed, so when it came time to try something new and creative, cake decorating topped the list. Conveniently, my husband's birthday was right around the corner. Ruth, the cake genius, agreed to teach me how to decorate his birthday cake.

I arrived at her house to find the cake sitting on a piece of covered cardboard, the crumb coat already applied. This is a thin layer of frosting applied before the serious decorating begins. It prevents the top layer of the cake from breaking away while applying the frosting and keeps the cake fresh in case you can't decorate it right away. Mind blown already.

Ray loves to camp, hike, canoe, and bike, so the decorating theme was easy. I ordered a cake decoration set, including a light-up tent, campfire, and canoe and paddle. I also found a small tool in the shape of a bike that looks much like the electric bike he just bought. Sweetland, our favorite candy store, sells chocolate candy in the shape of tiny rocks, which was perfect. Ruth threw in a pine tree, broken pretzels that looked like logs, and small peanut butter cups for tree stumps.

"You really can't mess up too bad," she said before starting. "You can always fix it with more frosting." This was heartening.

The first step, she said, is deciding what you want to do. I pictured a lake, a bike path, and a camping spot. Once we figured out the general configuration, she used a spatula to cut three shallow lines to mark the water, path, and land. Next came coloring the frosting for the separate sections, applying it liberally, and standing back for a good look. The brown bike path needed sparkly sugar to look like sand. We placed the tent, bike, and campfire, then the canoe, the tree, and the rocks.

Once we had everything in place, we stood back again to see what was missing. More rocks added, little frosting grass piped on between the rocks and around the water's edge. I thought it was magnificent, but Ruth said we weren't done yet. She then used white frosting to pipe around the top edge of the cake and the base as well. Now it was finished, and it was perfect. The best cake I had ever decorated in my life.

The birthday cake was a huge hit the next day, Ray's birthday, as the extended family gasped and exclaimed as I ceremoniously set it down it from of him. Even Ray was impressed, especially by the cool tool in the shape of a bike. Most of the cake was gone by the end of the party, which is the whole point of a cake. Eat and enjoy.

LESSONS LEARNED:

1. Ask the expert. Ruth has decorated probably thousands of cakes over the years. She knew what she was doing and was happy to share her expertise.

2. Have the right tools. A pliable and thin spatula, frosting bags and tips, and a variety of tubs and bowls for frosting are necessary.

3. Mistakes are fixable. Frosting is the great covering for all cake-decorating errors. Just add more and the flaw disappears.

4. Be generous. I tended to hold back on my frosting use, but Ruth encouraged me to use more. She was right; it doesn't pay to skimp on frosting.

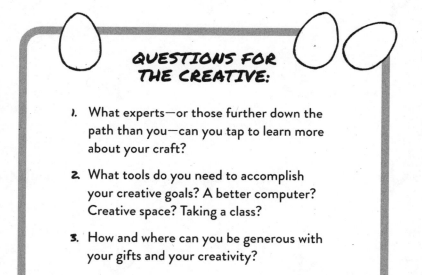

QUESTIONS FOR THE CREATIVE:

1. What experts—or those further down the path than you—can you tap to learn more about your craft?

2. What tools do you need to accomplish your creative goals? A better computer? Creative space? Taking a class?

3. How and where can you be generous with your gifts and your creativity?

CHAPTER NINE

EGGING ON THE GIFT OF CREATIVITY

THE CHICKENS

One of the very best thing about chickens (besides the delightful and often curious company) is the gift of their eggs. Our chickens lay glorious brown eggs that range from light tan to brownish red, from smallish to alarmingly large, from more pointed on one end to nice and fat in the middle. Some are a bit speckled, some look like the color was painted on, and many are absolutely perfect in shape and color.

Only once in all these years have I had a double-yolked egg, but every single yolk is a deep orange-yellow. The color of a burning sunset, a blood orange, a gorgeous daylily. I could go on about the beauty of a perfect egg yolk, not to mention the taste of good, toasted bread dipped into an over-easy fried egg.

Eggs come in a variety of sizes and colors, though if you buy eggs at the grocery store you might think every egg is white and the same size. Most of the time, any egg that isn't white or obviously another color is called "brown" by nonchicken people. But eggs range from white to cream, blue, pink, green, tan, brown, and a deep chocolate brown, depending on the breed.

Cream Legbars, Araucanas, and Ameraucanas lay blue eggs; the mixed-breed Easter Eggers lay green eggs; Welsummers, Barnevelders, and Marans lay dark brown eggs; Leghorns lay white eggs. Yet for all the variety on the outside, eggs are all the same on the inside, and taste is determined not by shell color but by what the hen eats. Hens who eat a diet high in grasses, vegetables, seeds, and herbs have better tasting eggs. There is just something about eggs laid by chickens who are able to roam the yard snacking on greenery.

Folks often wonder if fresh eggs—and by fresh I mean straight from the chicken—need to be refrigerated. The answer is no, if you don't wash them. Eggs are laid with a thin coating over them that prevents bacteria and air from getting in through the porous shells, which allows them to stay fresh longer. The eggs can sit in a beautiful bowl on your counter for a couple of weeks if you haven't washed them.

To be perfectly honest, chickens aren't all that careful about where they poop, and sometimes they poop where they lay. Which means eggs can have poop on them. They might have dirt on them. We've even seen blood on a few eggs if the hen has an issue with her vent. If you don't want poopy eggs on your counter,

> "THERE ARE DAYS WHEN I AM ENVIOUS OF MY HENS, WHEN I HUNGER FOR A PURPOSE AS PERFECT AND SURE AS A SINGLE DAILY EGG."
> —BARBARA KINGSOLVER

wash them and put them in the refrigerator. No big deal. They'll keep for months. Probably, if you've bought fresh eggs from a farmer's market or roadside stand, they've been washed (see above) so refrigerate to be safe.

Healthy chickens lead to good eggs. And *Storey's Guide to Raising Chickens* by Gail Damerow describes the eight signs of a healthy chicken just to help us out. These include their appearance ("perky and alert"); activity level; production (the rate of egg laying); weight; odor (a healthy flock has a "characteristic odor"); and droppings (Who knew there are two different kinds of chicken poop, both healthy?).

Relatively rare in backyard flocks is disease, which is reassuring, but there are myriad ways for a chicken to be sick, thanks to various bacteria, viruses, molds, parasites, poisoning, defects at birth, and poor nutrition. Some diseases are serious enough to have to be reported to federal or state governments. This isn't the place to go into the gory details, but suffice to say that chickens can get sick and die. Sometimes a chicken dies for no apparent reason. When she does, bury her and mourn her passing, honoring her for the good food she provided each time she laid that perfect egg—as well as for the companionship her gentle self provided.

THE CREATIVE

If you've ever watched a hen preparing to lay an egg, you know that this is serious business. She determines the perfect laying spot, settles in with much fluffing and clucking, and then sits there, quite intentionally, until the job is done. She then announces to the world that she has *laid an egg*.

Living a creative life takes those same two things: determination and intentionality, according to Don Perini, professor of creativity and innovation and director of the Creativity and Innovation Honors Institute at Cornerstone University. Cornerstone is the only school in the nation at this point that offers a degree in creativity and innovation, though other institutions have classes in creativity and offer degrees in entrepreneurship and collaborative design.

Perini has built a life of teaching creativity and living creatively. He debunks the myth that only a select few are born creative. "The truth is, we're all creative," he said. "Creativity is a choice; it's a way of living."

The "way of living" Perini describes isn't a list of dos and don'ts or a prescription to be filled in order to become creative. In fact, he opens his book *Emerge*, written to help readers unleash their creativity, with these words in the introduction:

> If you are looking for a fast and easy way to unleash your creative potential, then this book, I am sorry to say, is not for you. If you desire to develop creative habits without much effort, if you are seeking a simple formula that will develop your unique talents, you will be disappointed to learn that I have nothing to teach you. I don't believe in the existence of a simple formula or step-by-step process for cultivating creativity.

Not the best way to sell a book, perhaps, but his point is a good one: we're all creative in our own ways, and creative habits open the door to creative outcomes. By allowing space for creativity, creativity emerges.

Creative habits include fashioning a space to do creative work. When I was finally able to have my own office, I decorated with stuff I love. There's the Carrot Top Paper Shop banner featuring literary heroines and literary quotes, photos of my family, books on writing, and a gorgeous three-drawer paper tray made by my father-in-law.

Some creatives work every day in a different coffee shop, some in a makerspace (sometimes called a hackerspace); others head off to a cabin in the woods to think. My friend Scott, an instructor for online university and PhD-level classes, literally travels the country with his laptop, checking in with his students while visiting the Grand Canyon, canoeing at the Boundary Waters, or hiking up a mountain in Washington State.

Another creative habit is allowing yourself idea-friendly times when your mind is free to create. This can be hard for some of us who live by deadlines and to-do lists and a whole lot of "I should

"NOISE PROVES NOTHING. OFTEN A HEN WHO HAS MERELY LAID AN EGG CACKLES AS IF SHE HAS LAID AN ASTEROID."
—MARK TWAIN

be doing this or that" sort of thinking. But if you can give yourself time to create, you may be surprised. I've found such time while walking the track at the gym, sitting on my swing in the back yard, walking outside, and just sitting on the deck, soaking up the sun.

Activities, places, and books also feed our creative life. Charity Singleton Craig, author with Ann Kroeker of *On Being a Writer: 12 Simple Habits for a Writing Life That Lasts*, describes a time when she was overwhelmed as a newlywed with three new stepsons. She found herself writing only about marriage and motherhood yet yearned for more.

She asked her husband, "Would you be interested, or at least willing, to go to an exhibit at the art museum Saturday?" He agreed.

"On Saturday we drove to the art museum and not only took in the Ai Weiwei exhibit but also became members of the museum, a commitment from both of us that we would surround ourselves with what inspires me to write. It worked. Within a couple of weeks, I wrote on my blog about that conversation we had in the kitchen, submitted a review of the exhibit to *Tweetspeak Poetry*, and planned two more articles based on the museum membership."

In the following short excerpt from Kroeker and Craig's *On Being a Writer*, I substituted "creating" for "writing": "Evaluate your world: what one thing can you change this week—the things you read, the places you go, the hobbies you enjoy, the conversations you engage in, etc.—that will connect with what you currently are [*creating*] or hope to [*create*]? Make that change."

Creative habits also include having what Perini calls a "capture machine," which is simply a way to record your ideas. This can be a bedside pad of paper, a recording device, a diary, the notes app on your smartphone. Creative people save their ideas immediately, lest they be forgotten. Some people even have a waterproof notepad for the shower for those ideas that pop up as they soap up.

Perini, who naturally allows himself plenty of opportunities for his creative self to bloom, defines creativity as "using the whole brain to come up with something new and useful." He adds, "You can choose to complain or create. Keep going, keep falling forward. Ask yourself how you are growing and what can you do differently. Creatives become masters of failure, too." Try again. Keep trying. And keep trying again and again.

Of course, there are many things that hinder our creative impulses. Perini listed resistance, fear, self-doubt, procrastination, victimization,

> **"MAKING ART IS ALMOST CERTAINLY AN ACT OF BRAVERY."**
> —ALL THAT IS MADE BY ALABASTER

busyness, perfectionism. There are probably a few more floating around out there, and you may have a few to add. *All That Is Made: A Guide to Faith and the Creative Life* was created by Alabaster, a maker group of highly designed books and print media. The book includes a discussion of three barriers creatives must face as they move into their work: "I need to be perfect." "It needs to be perfect." "The message needs to be perfect." All are barriers to be breached when building a creative life and practice.

"Our message will be messy because we are messy. . . . Let things unfold, and let them be what they become," said Alabaster.

It's about letting yourself breathe, relax, see where an idea goes. When one of my sons was about four years old, I was helping him go to the bathroom after church when I discovered he was wearing no underwear.

"Where are your underpants?" I asked, aghast, and at some decibel.

Without missing a beat, he said, "Oh, I'm letting my skin breathe."

My first thought was, *How did he come up with that answer so quickly?* and my second thought was, *That's not an unreasonable idea. I imagine he felt quite free all morning, and sometimes, you just have to let yourself breathe.* So, too, in creativity. Breathe, relax, enjoy, and let the ideas flow.

A few years ago, Don Perini spoke at the Breathe conference about the creative process. He said many good and useful things, and I bought his book *Emerge.* But what sticks with me still is his emphasis on how fostering good creative habits will help build a creative process, and from that process, "Something will emerge." He was so emphatic in getting this group of faith-based creatives to trust the work of creative habits that he had the whole group yelling, "Something will emerge!" by the end of his talk.

With intentionality and determination, as Perini said, habits designed to foster creativity and an openness to the creative process, something will emerge. Whether it's a piece of art, a tasty new dessert, a gorgeous quilt, a life-changing sermon, an innovative solution to houselessness, or a perfect brown egg, something will emerge.

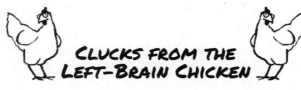

CLUCKS FROM THE LEFT-BRAIN CHICKEN

This chapter is meaty (beef meaty, not chicken meaty). We come to the very heart of living a creative life: the act of creating something requires powerful will, breathing space, courage, and imagination. All difficult things, but when we commit to the supportive habits (for me, a nice green yard, good grains to eat, and a stellar coop), creating comes as natural as, well, laying an egg. It's who you are.

1. The heart of every creative endeavor is the idea. Develop your own "capture machine" to record your ideas as they come to you. For ideas on what your capture machine could be, review suggestions in this chapter.

2. Pay attention to what gets you in the mindset of creating. Is it taking a walk, lighting a candle, rereading your favorite poem, going to a museum? Using these sparks, build a creative habit that fits you. Remember, there isn't a guaranteed formula, but there are ways to encourage your creativity to emerge.

3. Breathe. Relax. Laugh. Enjoy.

Broody Thoughts

- Describe what "something will emerge" means to you and to your creative life.

- What kind of capture machine will work best for you to record your brilliant ideas?

- List all the things that you think are holding you back from a truly creative life. Now list possible solutions to those things (including stuff like getting a new job, resigning from that committee, seeing a therapist).

- What new and useful thing do you dream about creating?

- List ten creative ideas for your new project. Now list ten more.

Birds of a Feather

Storey's Guide to Raising Chickens: Care, Feeding, Facilities by Gail Damerow (Storey Publishing)

Emerge by Don Perini (Pot-Boilers)

All That Is Made: A Guide to Faith and the Creative Life (Alabaster)

Creativity, Inc.: Overcoming the Unseen Forces That Stand in the Way of True Inspiration by Ed Catmull, with Amy Wallace (Random House)

CHAPTER TEN

CARE AND KEEPING OF THE FLOCK

THE CHICKENS

Chickens have a lot of enemies. Lacy Finn Borgo, the author of *All Will Be Well*, had chickens killed by bobcats. And one time she saw an eagle make off with one of her turkeys, but the turkey was too fat for the eagle to carry. My son's fiancée, Olivia, walked out to her chicken coop and found a hawk trapped in the coop by a protective net (which obviously didn't work) and one fatality. Name them: racoons, opossums, skunks, snakes, eagles, hawks, dogs, foxes, coyotes, wolves—basically anything that eats meat has tried to break into a coop. Hence, the importance of creating a home for your chickens that keeps them safe from predators.

Not that the circle of life doesn't go both ways. Our chickens once trapped a mouse against the wall of the garage, where it was pecked until its untimely end. Chickens will kill snakes, rats, and even scorpions, plus eat worms, butterflies, caterpillars, and all manner of insects. And of course we know chickens will do it to themselves too. One of our batches of chicks included a rooster, which we couldn't keep. A rooster is loud and aggressive, but we didn't want to kill the bird just because we didn't know what else to do with him. Before we had a plan, he solved that problem himself by making the bad decision to visit a neighbor with a dog.

Keeping chickens can be as easy or complicated as you make it. Basic knowledge of feed for chicks and older hens isn't rocket science; create your coop out of scrap lumber and chicken wire, but make sure the coop protects from predators that can dive in from the top or dig in underneath the fence; clean water is easy; and heated water dispensers are wonderful in the winter.

For the most part, chickens are low-maintenance with a high return in eggs (and meat if you choose meat hens). What's even better is that chickens come back to their roost every night when the sun goes down. Without fail, our flock wanders from whatever corner of the yard they're in right into their coop. Every evening I marvel at how God made chickens and that we don't have to chase or lure them into the coop. They just go, clucking softly and ready for a good night's rest.

The spring 2020 issue of *Guide to Backyard Chickens* featured an article titled "What to Do About Poultry Remorse." Apparently, poultry remorse is a thing, probably a lot like all the puppy remorse going on during the COVID-19 pandemic: "Oops, got a puppy when I was lonely and home all the time, but

> **"IF YOU DREAM OF BECOMING AN EAGLE, YOU FOLLOW YOUR DREAMS AND NOT THE WORDS OF A BUNCH OF CHICKENS."**
> **—PENNY JOHNSON JERALD**

now I'm back in the office and don't know what to do with the dang dog that keeps chewing up the furniture."

Love chickens and reading about them, and now considering a little gathering? This helpful article on poultry remorse by Rachel Yoder listed five things to consider before acquiring a backyard flock:

1. Choose the right breed—consider size, activity level, friendliness.
2. Create the right home—consider accessibility, size, and whether you want portability or not.
3. Choose the right litter—sand is cheap and easy to clean and cuts down on accumulated moisture.
4. Feed cheaply—save money by letting them range around the yard and saving table scraps and garden extras.
5. Know basic first aid—keep Epsom salts, hydrogen peroxide, antibiotic ointment, and petroleum jelly on hand.

I am hardly a helicopter chicken mom. I'm certainly not a helicopter dog mom, unlike my niece, who puts foot pad moisturizer on her dogs regularly. I'm barely a helicopter human mom! I once sent my kid to school with a broken foot after she tripped off the front porch. "Walk it off," I said as she hobbled, crying, to the bus stop. In my defense, this kid had had two negative x-rays on various body parts in the previous year. And yes, I got her from school an hour and a half later and took her in for an x-ray. I even advocated for a boot, not crutches, so she wouldn't slip on the wet, cement floor at school. A+ for me.

As for the dog, I'm resentful that she needs a walk when we have a perfectly good backyard to run around in. If it weren't for my husband and daughter, the animals in our world would probably go hungry and live in filth. Kid 4's room is foul, but he's old enough to clean it himself, and if he wants to live in a garbage dump, that's fine with me. We'll tear up the carpet when he moves out.

Yet it was me who bought the head of cabbage, talked my husband into drilling a hole through it, and helped him hang it in the coop to keep the chickens entertained during the long winter when they're stuck inside. As I wrote about before, the girls love it and are now going on their fourth cabbage. The xylophone my niece recently gifted me for the coop is also installed in the

"YOU ARE NOT KEEPING THEM, OF COURSE, TO MAKE OR EVEN TO SAVE MONEY. YOU ARE NOT KEEPING THEM AS PETS. YOU ARE KEEPING THEM FOR THE SIMPLE PLEASURE OF THEIR COMPANY AND THE BEAUTY AND TASTINESS OF THEIR EGGS AND THEIR MEAT. YOU ARE RAISING THEM BECAUSE YOU WANT TO STRIKE A MODEST BLOW FOR THE LIBERATION OF THE CHICKEN—AND, INDEED, OF ALL LIVING THINGS ON EARTH."
—CHARLES DANIEL AND PAGE SMITH, THE CHICKEN BOOK

winter coop, and I wouldn't say no to a chicken swing in the coop either. Am I paying top dollar for these things? Nope. Chickens don't care about fancy; they care about the solid basics.

That's what I like about chickens. They are easy to care for—way easier than cows, pigs, horses, goats, sheep, and human children—charming, and fun to get to know and hang out with. A little care and love goes a long way with a chicken and toward giving it a very good life.

THE CREATIVE

The care and keeping of your creative life may not be as much physical work as taking care of chickens, but there are some marked similarities. Our creative life needs protection so it can be safe and thrive, it must be fed, maintenance is important, and a basic understanding of the needs of the creative heart is vital.

> **"NO MATTER WHAT YOUR AGE, PROFESSION, OR PERSONAL INTERESTS, YOU NEED CREATIVITY IN YOUR LIFE."**
> —Tanner Christensen, The Creativity Challenge

A while back, I became interested in the Enneagram system, dipping into Richard Rohr's *The Enneagram: A Christian Perspective* and *The Road Back to You: An Enneagram Journey to Self-Discovery* by Ian Morgan Cron and Suzanne Stabile. I even worked through Enneagram coach Beth McCord's *Enneagram Type 7* interactive guide.

It came as no surprise to those who know me that I am a 7, one of the three numbers (5, 6, 7) in the Fear Triad. Sevens are generally glass-half-full people, usually in good moods, good at multitasking, curious, like variety and trying new things, aren't afraid of meeting new people. Lots of freelance writers—who can jump from project to project with ease—are 7s. Bored with one story? Work on another! Email a complete stranger and ask them to be part of your book? No problem.

Yet 7s can have a hard time finishing a project, hate being controlled, easily blame others for their problems. We can flit about without settling on anything or anyone. And we're driven by the need to protect ourselves. "These numbers are driven by fear—Five externalizes it, Six internalizes it, and Seven forgets it," according to Cron and Stabile.

Rohr describes 7s this way: "Relaxed, full of good humor, imaginative, sunny, playful, with a disarming kind of charm—until one day they notice that all this also serves to protect them from anxiety and pain."

Who knew? Not me. I would rather ignore a hard thing than face it. Yes, there is a broken vacuum sitting in my living room right this minute. I'm annoyed that it broke after a year, and somehow think it will miraculously fix itself. Meanwhile, the state of the floor is degenerating quickly.

Just knowing that I tend to hide from and avoid hard things has helped me stop avoiding them. By understanding myself and my tendencies, I can better care for myself. I started going to a therapist in early 2019 after a really crummy 2018. In that one year my dad, in extremely touch-and-go fragile health, ended up in a nursing home; one kid was making a series of very bad choices for which he entered the justice system; I was writing a difficult piece on sexual harassment, for which I talked to a number of victims, the heartbreak of which was traumatizing; a person I considered a close friend suddenly challenged me in a way that felt like a personal attack; and a bad mammogram led to caught-very-early breast cancer complete with two lumpectomies and radiation. I totally needed a therapist!

Now, several years later, my dad is still living, and we go to the library and lunch every other week or so. My son is in college studying to be a history teacher. The breast cancer is gone. And I continue to see my therapist every other week, which helps me better understand myself, my circumstances, and the other humans in my life. Without the work I do with her, I wouldn't be writing this book today. I'd still be avoiding the pain that might come with rejection.

Taking Care of Creativity

Creativity needs nurturing and creatives need care. That care will look different for every person, but the basics remain the same. First, you need shelter and protection from the elements and predators. Do you have safe people who love you, who aren't in competition with you, and who will tell you when you're off track or just being a jerk?

I asked my niece Kelsey to read several of the early chapters of this book. I'm sure it wasn't easy for her to say, "Annie, you need to add more of yourself in here," or "Some transitions would be good," but she did it anyway and naturally she was right. My friend, novelist Tracy Groot, has several beta readers for each novel and she begs them to be honest about what needs work. And they are. She trusts them to be honest and they trust her not to throw a fit when they point out something that needs work.

Other safe places can be a friend group that has nothing to do with your creative endeavor but that loves you and protects you; family members who are safe and who love you without expectation; a like-minded group of creatives who encourage and appropriately challenge. Search out the people who protect you, as well as develop the skills to protect yourself from the barbs of life.

Second, creatives need to be fed. Dark chocolate is wonderful, but so is an activity that challenges the mind and opens the door to creative thinking. Some people are fed by being with people; others are fed by being alone. Some creatives are the life of the party while others sit against the wall and try not to make eye contact with anyone. The point is to find what feeds your creativity and engage in those activities from time to time.

In Tanner Christensen's book *The Creativity Challenge*, on offer are creative activities for everyone, 150 challenges divided into five modes of thinking: convergent, divergent, lateral, aesthetic, and emergent. Some of his challenges include setting a timer for fifteen minutes and do something boring; gather craft materials and spend ten minutes making something basic like a hat; listen to a work by Mozart.

My daughter, the Left-Brain Chicken, recently took a six-week beginner drawing class as a new way to explore her creativity. My other daughter loves true crime shows and her crazy pets as a form of creative expression. My husband loves winter camping and long bike rides. I love reading *Bridgerton* and Jack Reacher, puzzling, fishing, a good party, and any of the Great Lakes. We are all fed in different ways. Find what feeds you and partake to avoid starving your creative self. Once you are filled, your creativity will find a way to pour out.

Third, general maintenance is necessary for a vibrant creative life. Get enough sleep, eat well, exercise, work on your mental health, brush and floss your teeth, take your prescribed medications, get yearly checkups, don't skip your mammogram, treat others like you would like to be treated, remember daily that the center of the universe isn't you (a scientific fact, BTW).

One of my daughters has a nasty autoimmune disease for which she takes a crap ton of medication. Recently she told me that once in a great while she doesn't take her medications so she can pretend she's not sick for a day. She admits that she pays big the next day with pain through the roof. Her medications help her maintain a pain-free life in the midst of a nasty disease. I understand her thinking because I think the same way about exercise and sleep, but we both know that good maintenance is important and necessary.

Your creative self is ignored at the expense of your art, whether your art is cooking, architecture, sewing, writing, painting, or woodworking. Feeding one feeds the other. I may be proficient at avoiding things I don't like, but I've learned that basic care and maintenance means increased creativity and a much better life.

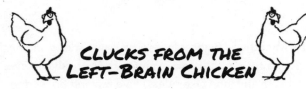

CLUCKS FROM THE LEFT-BRAIN CHICKEN

Ann takes good care of me and the flock. But a hen knows her own self best, and I know when I need self-care. When I feel hot and bothered, I treat myself to a heavenly dust bath. I have a chat with Sadie when I'm feeling down because she is the best listener. When I'm bored, I tease Tipper the dog until she chases me and then watch and laugh as she gets in trouble. Prioritize taking care of yourself.

1. Evaluate your general maintenance. Is there anything you can work on? Better sleep, healthier eating habits, exercise?

2. In the next two weeks, do something that nourishes you. Sign up for a drawing class, go to the library, take a day hike, have a coffee date with a friend.

3. Spend time with yourself. I know this sounds cheesy, but how will you know what you need if you don't listen to and learn about yourself?

BROODY THOUGHTS

- What are you doing to feed your creative life? Or are you starving it, and why?

- If you haven't done so already, read up on the Enneagram and determine your Enneagram number. What traits of your number do you identify with most?

- What general life maintenance areas do you need to work on? Make the appointments, join the gym, and start going to sleep earlier.

- What things stymie your creativity? Certain people? Too much time playing games on your phone? The endless news cycle? What can you eliminate?

Birds of a Feather

The Road Back to You: An Enneagram Journey to Self-Discovery by Ian Morgan Cros and Suzanne Stabile

The Creativity Challenge: Design, Experiment, Test, Innovate, Build, Create, Inspire, and Unleash Your Genius by Tanner Christensen

Take Joy: A Book for Writers by Jane Yolen

CREATIVE EGG–TIVITY #5
DRAWING CHICKENS

When you know an author and illustrator with six books published by one of the top children's book publishers, naturally you ask him to help you learn to draw a chicken. Kenneth Kraegel looked a little nonplussed when I plopped down next to him at the Breathe conference and said, "So, Ken, can you help me learn to draw a chicken?" He can draw dragons and emus, I reasoned; why not a chicken? He acquiesced to my odd request.

We agreed that I would draw ten different chickens and send him pictures, which I (less than) promptly did. My efforts ranged from very basic, which I copied from my great-niece Adeline's very cute chicken drawings, to quite elaborate, which I drew based on a *How to Draw Birds* guide. He liked the variety of styles, then told me to pick the one I liked best and focus on that, drawing a whole bunch more chickens like it.

I found a lot of reasons to not draw chickens, including, but not limited to, having to write this book, not having the exact right drawing paper, and other important stuff like going to the library. Finally, being the deadline-conscious girl I am, I got busy drawing beaks and whole chickens. I liked watching my beaks develop as I drew pages of them. I figured out that previous chicken drawings were missing the wattle, and I made the wings bigger on the new batch of chickens. I sent another ten or so drawings to him.

Kraegel responded thus: "Your chickens have really developed! They are unambiguously chickens, and they have the beginnings of real personality. If you want to go further, you could develop these chickens into three distinct characters or moods. Or you could use some of your existing drawings and go over them again and again in pencil, smoothing out the lines and seeing how little changes to the line alter the feel of the drawing. By loosely going over and over a drawing, I often find little ways to improve it and it ends up feeling more solid."

That paragraph is instructional gold for budding illustrators. It tells me that I can learn to draw a chicken, but that it takes practice and intentionality. "You can learn to draw. It's a matter of breaking things down into shapes, then draw those shapes, then smooth it out," he said when we talked.

He also mentioned playing to his strengths. He doesn't draw people very well, but he loves to draw fuzzy little animals, so his books are full of those. His newest is full of mushrooms, snails, ladybugs, and butterflies. Kraegel also mentioned Maurice Sendak, whose most famous book, *Where the Wild Things Are*, didn't start out that way. It started as "Where the Wild Horses Are," but Sendak didn't think he could draw horses well. Over several years, *Where the Wild Things Are* emerged. Sendak, too, played to his strengths and it paid off.

Drawing chickens will never be my strength. Drawing anything will not be my strength, but I can break a creative project down into its basic shapes, create those shapes, and connect them smoothly. Perfecting a piece of writing requires the same steps when it comes to sentences, paragraphs, sections, and chapters.

Interestingly, when my daughter and niece read several of these chapters, they commented that a few transitions might be needed. I've written news stories for years, not always the best place to add smooth transitions, due to lack of space and low word counts. About the same time they were reading the chapters, I got in the mail, from a person I wouldn't have expected, a copy of an editorial I wrote as a college senior right before graduation. It was about the transitions we face in life. Who knew that back in 1984 I was dealing with transitions too.

I began looking more closely at transitions in my writing, at taking the basic shapes of paragraphs and sections and smoothing them out, filling them in, and creating a cohesive whole. Creativity in one part of life, as usual, impacts all areas of life. Hopefully I'm in the process of moving smoothly into life as a more creative person thanks to a few drawings of chickens.

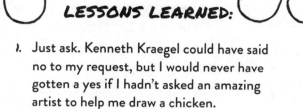

LESSONS LEARNED:

1. Just ask. Kenneth Kraegel could have said no to my request, but I would never have gotten a yes if I hadn't asked an amazing artist to help me draw a chicken.

2. Recognize resistance. I resisted drawing because I knew I wasn't good at it, but according to Kraegel, I was making progress. Move through the resistance and watch your creativity grow.

3. Follow your creative path. Kraegel could still be making awful music (see chapter 11), but he veered from that dream to what he truly loves and is good at: writing and illustrating books.

4. Make the transition. Whether drawing chickens, writing a book, or moving from one dream to another, creatives know that moving ahead in life and on a project requires step-by-step transitions that may be difficult but are necessary.

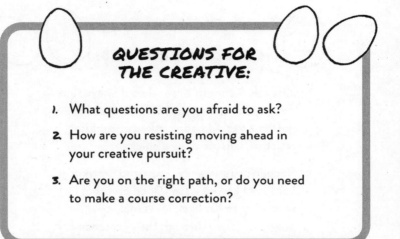

QUESTIONS FOR THE CREATIVE:

1. What questions are you afraid to ask?

2. How are you resisting moving ahead in your creative pursuit?

3. Are you on the right path, or do you need to make a course correction?

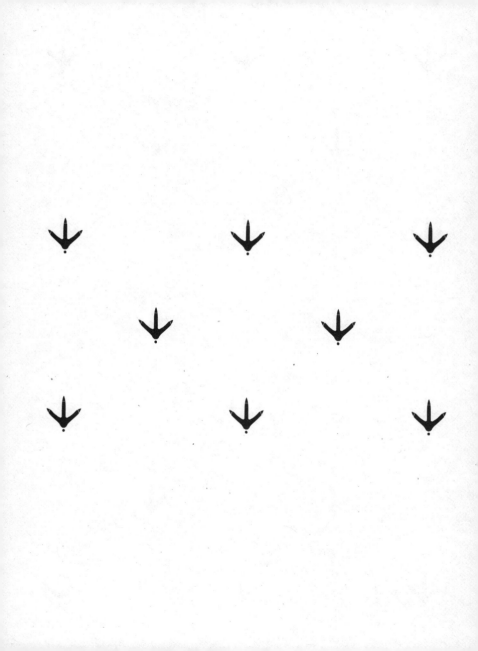

CHAPTER ELEVEN

THE BUSINESS END OF A CHICKEN

THE CHICKENS

The website for the American Poultry Association (APA) is a revelation. If you go there, you'll see that poultry people are serious about their birds. The APA's mission is "to promote and protect standard-bred poultry in all its phases," through publication of the American Standard of Perfection, encouraging and promoting poultry shows, and granting licenses to those who judge at poultry shows.

Lists of poultry associations and clubs are provided, a schedule of poultry-related events includes the Utah Fancy Poultry Association—Spring Double Show and a Cornish Seminar, and articles provide useful information on poultry photography, specific breeds, topics related to raising chicks, incubation, transport cages, and the oddly specific "Artificial Insemination in Cochin Bantams."

Membership is twenty dollars annually for adult and junior members, but joining for three years nets you a ten-dollar discount. Cost is double for those outside of the United States and Canada. The list of accepted breeds and varieties on the website numbers 529. This includes turkeys; light, medium, and heavy ducks and geese; guineas;

and all manner of chickens, including Single Comb, Clean-Legged (SCCL), Rose Comb, Clean-Legged (RCCL), All Other Comb, Clean-Legged (AOCCL), and Featherlegs.

Breed names range from exotic (Dominique, Sumatra, Cubalaya) to commonplace (New Hampshire, Sussex, Hamburg) to downright odd (Dorking, Sicilian Buttercup, Naked Neck).

Chickens not only are divided by comb and leg coverings but by size as well. Bantam chickens are miniature chickens ranging from a fifth to two-thirds the size of standard birds, with lots of standard breeds having bantam counterparts. Eggs are commensurately smaller. All in all, bantams are cute little things and often quite sweet, according to the experts.

Chicken owners can choose whether they want laying hens, meat hens, hens that are good for both, or the fancy, ornamental breeds that make you stare in wonder at the beauty and downright craziness of God's creation, not to mention question the wisdom of breeders. The Polish White gives new meaning to "bad hair day." The Polish Frizzle's head looks like a mushroom cloud, while the Brabanter has a U-shaped comb that makes her look demonic.

We didn't go for the exotic around here. We chose four standard buff Orpington laying hens, which are an English

"MY SWEET SPOT IS WHERE MY PASSION, ETHICS, AND ABUNDANCE ALL MEET."
—FLORA BOWLEY, YOUR CREATIVE WORK SPACE

SCCL breed engineered by William Cook of Orpington in Kent, England, in the 1880s. He was looking for a practical meat and egg bird. His buff Orpingtons were preceded by black Orpingtons and followed by white, blue, and splash Orpingtons, though buff remains the most popular. Cook's Orpingtons were hugely popular in England and within a decade also popular in the United States.

We also have one gray girl with a bright red comb. The bin at Family Farm & Home said the chick was a Barred (alternating dark and light-striped feathers) Rock, also called a Barred Plymouth Rock, one of the oldest breeds in the United States, and "almost single-handedly responsible for keeping meat, protein, and eggs in the American diet through the time of rationing" during World War II, according to The Happy Chicken Coop (www.thehappychickencoop.com).

> **"ANYBODY DEPENDING ON SOMEBODY ELSE'S GODS IS DEPENDING ON A FOX NOT TO EAT CHICKENS."**
> —ZORA NEALE HURSTON

I'm not so sure. It wouldn't be the first time a chick was in the wrong bin. I'm leaning toward Sal (named for the little girl in the classic children's book *Blueberries for Sal*) being a blue Orpington, but I'm no chicken classifier. Whatever she is, we love her.

We chose the buff Orpingtons because we knew them from when my son's sixth-grade class raised them. They are good girls, good layers, and quite cheerful. We chose the blue—actually, I didn't choose her. My kids rushed out and got me two new chicks when a visiting dog killed one of the buffs. Like within an hour.

Eggs of a Different Color

Eggs are another determinant when it comes to choosing hens. Different breeds lay different colored eggs. In one of the odder facts about chickens, the color of the eggs can often be determined by the color of the hen's ear lobes. A white ear lobe means white eggs; a brown or reddish-brown ear lobe means brown eggs; blue lobes mean blue eggs. This isn't 100 percent true for every breed (Silkies, for instance, have blue lobes but lay white eggs), but it's pretty close. It's about the color of pigment the hen has in her body, which is a whole separate discussion involving big words like *biliverdin* and *protoporphyrin* and way beyond my grasp of hen physiology. Suffice to say, there is much to consider when considering chickens.

Michelle Franks put as much effort into choosing her nine hens as she put into her investment industry job. Her dream was seeing a variety of colored eggs each day, so she picked her breeds carefully. She has Leghorns named Snow White and Hazel; a Plymouth Blue Rock named Liz Taylor; a Pearl Leghorn named Butterscotch; an Easter Egger called Farrah Fawcett; an

> *"CREATIVE SELF-EXPRESSION, IN ITS MANY FORMS, CAN BE A PARTICULARLY POWERFUL MEANS OF COPING WITH LIFE'S INEVITABLE CHALLENGES."*
> —SCOTT BARRY KAUFMAN AND CAROLYN GREGOIRE, WIRED TO CREATE: UNRAVELING THE MYSTERIES OF THE CREATIVE MIND

Olive Egger named Dionne Warwick; a Crested Cream Legbar named Gigi; a Fresh Copper Maran named Mabel, and a lavender Orpington christened Laverne.

She gets light brown eggs, white, bluish-green, dark-chocolate brown, cream, olive, and sometimes pink eggs. Michelle loves every one of her girls, crediting them with helping give her life new meaning at the start of the pandemic. She traveled often for her job selling investment products to firms and clients, but the pandemic shut down travel, leaving her working from home and alone. She started with five chicks, which she brooded in her dining room.

"I sang a good morning song to them and had my coffee while talking to them. They were something I could take care of when everything else was out of control," said Michelle.

She soon sold her home in a fancy subdivision and bought three acres with a plan to re-create the experiences she had as a child on relatives' farms. She tore down the boring ranch house on the property and built a farmhouse and chicken coop in the middle of the three acres. She added four more birds.

"My industry was rewarding, but it's not tangible. I remember the simple life of my relatives, remember them being happy, and wanted to recreate that," said Michelle, who in 2022 left her job in the investment industry and, as of this writing, is deciding on her next move.

She knows just what she's doing with her chickens, though. She used hardware cloth for the fenced run, having the builders bury it deep under the concrete slab on which her roofed coop sits. She has an electronic door that closes at night and opens in the morning, keeping her chickens inside the coop in case a predator finds its way into the run. She has a pellet rifle at the ready should need arise. She sings to the hens in the morning and sits with them in the coop each evening.

"Chickens make me happy. They are happy. They ground me and bring me back to the present," Michelle said. "They give me a reason to smile. I am happier and more satisfied and get more joy out of cleaning the coop than with anything I've done in my professional life."

She chose wisely.

THE CREATIVE

Raising chickens is a long-term commitment in time, energy, and money, but with a high return in eggs, meat, well-being, and love. That same commitment and payoff occurs when you commit to your creative life. In both cases, decisions must be made to ensure success.

Creatives can consider several things. Is your creative life a hobby or a vocation? What is your niche or focus? How much time and money will you invest? What are your long-term and short-term goals? How will you balance your day job with your new creative goals?

It will surprise no one who knows me that I'm not a detailed planner. I like to call it macroplanning, as in "I'm going to do these three writing-related things today, go shopping in the afternoon, and have spaghetti for dinner." None of this, "At 9:10 a.m. I'll work on chapter 2; at 1:30 p.m. I'll edit chapter 1; at 5:10 p.m. I'll start dinner." In fact, I'm writing this chapter two days later than I planned because my dad called me as I was finishing up at the gym, concerned that my mom's birthday was approaching and he didn't have presents yet and could we set up a time in the next couple of days for me to help him get presents. I called him from the gym and said, "Be ready in five minutes."

We headed to my daughter's house to pick up her vacuum to borrow (you'll recall my mentioning ours has been broken for weeks. I just can't make myself buy a new one because it's only a year old and I loved that vacuum), then to Office Depot for an address book for my mom. No adequate address books, but Dad bought two reams of paper and a pack of yellow legal pads. Then Target, still no address book but two birthday cards purchased. Back across town to our all-time favorite candy store, Sweetland, for a box of chocolate for the birthday girl, a visit to Hallmark but still no address books, and, finally, "what the heck, we're out, we might as well have lunch too." Three hours later, I needed a nap. No writing, but precious time spent with my dad, in his mideighties, who won't be around forever.

The lesson here is that I created a freelance life that, for the most part, allows me the flexibility to take my father birthday shopping when he needs to. My husband and I decided that I would stay home with the children and build a freelance business while he started his teaching career. I was able to build a career writing for the local newspaper, a local magazine, and a national publication between taking kids to doctor appointments, attending school functions, and the seemingly endless list of things that must be done to feed and clothe children.

One key decision I made and continue to make: investing in a good computer. I used a Mac desktop for a number of years, then got an Apple laptop. I recently bought the new MacBook Pro with the M1 chip, which will last me for years. I want a computer I can depend on and am willing to spend money on it. Other business decisions included becoming an LLC, paying estimated taxes each quarter, and keeping track of expenses and mileage.

I asked Chris Morris, a CPA and creative (yes, they can coexist in one person), about the biggest mistake beginning creatives make. He said, "Not treating their endeavor like the business it is soon enough." I'm all in. I treat my writing as a business, though you may decide to enjoy your creative endeavor as a hobby, and that's fine too. Make the decision, after careful thought and research, for what is best for you and your circumstances, yet stay flexible, willing to change things up when it becomes necessary.

Creative Cooking Meets Business Sense

David Geisser is a leading European chef who has a passion for people and the culinary arts. He has trained at a number of gourmet restaurants across Switzerland, served for two years in the Swiss Guard in Rome, and opened Kochstudio, a cooking studio, in Wermatswil. He is the author of *The Vatican Cookbook: Presented by the Pontifical Swiss Guard*, which includes recipes for dishes served to Vatican dignitaries and guests, as well as favorite dishes of a number of popes.

His 2022 release is *The Lenten Cookbook*, which offers seventy-five international recipes centered on the Lenten season. This chef made the decision to expand out from the kitchen and into the business of cooking, an endeavor that takes both creativity and curiosity.

"Due to the fact that the business of cooking and gastronomy involves an enormously competitive environment, it is essential to show courage and plenty of creativity. Making the right decisions that not only satisfy the customers, but in the end fascinate and excite them with something and are best for the business takes a lot of courage every day," said Geisser. "These decisions are made more easily when one has a natural propensity for unbridled curiosity. In the end, this is the foundation for goal-oriented and ambitious work."

This extraordinary chef said that creativity is indispensable in making something that has never existed before and that courage is almost as important. "Lots of chefs tend to do the same thing over and over again, but only very few have the iron courage to think outside the box and do it with the risk that people might not like it," he said, adding that he nurtures his own creativity by staying on top of trends and products, reading about great personalities and creative chefs, and devouring good cookbooks.

He stepped outside the box with *The Lenten Cookbook*. "I wanted to create simple dishes which you can do without luxury items but that are still very tasty and contain exciting combinations," he said. "For me, Lent is a very exciting time, especially with regard to the Christian faith."

Geisser loves the whole process of creating excellent food. "There is a moment when you are still without an idea, then you discover a new herb or spice or maybe a new way of preparation, and everything starts rolling," he said. "You try different things, some work and others don't, but eventually something great comes out of it. The whole process is balm for the soul and a feeling of pure satisfaction when I have a beautiful result in the end."

Geisser makes decisions every day that bring life to his recipes, his vision, and his business. May we feed our creative selves the same way.

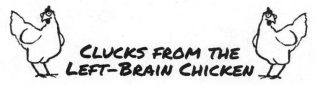

CLUCKS FROM THE LEFT-BRAIN CHICKEN

I don't pay taxes, being a chicken. I don't run my own business or sell my poop-impressionist art on Etsy. But I do understand about getting down to business. Sometimes things are uncomfortable or scary, but at the end of the day, you make the choice to move forward or you stay the same. Hmm, maybe I really should sell my poop art.

1. Think about your creative endeavor. Is it a hobby, a potential business, or a part-time side hustle? What decisions do you need to make to move forward on either of those paths?

2. Look at what you are already doing creatively. What steps can you take to push the project further? Example: additional art you can sell, podcast, book, nonprofit.

3. Make brave mini-decisions every time you start a creative session. Rewrite that sentence one more time to make it sing. Choose the more challenging subject to draw. Spend another fifteen minutes in your business brainstorm session and see what new things you come up with.

Broody Thoughts

- What decisions do you need to make regarding your creative life? Hobby or business? Full-time or part-time? Quit or keep your day job?

- What are your long- and short-term goals for a potential creative business?

- Build a business plan for your creative endeavor, including a summary of your business, description, market analysis, service or product you'll produce, marketing strategy, and financial projections. Do this even if you decide to keep it a hobby.

- Ponder Chris Morris's advice that people don't treat their creative activity like a business soon enough. How does that apply to you?

- How do the traits of curiosity and courage apply to the plan for your creative life?

Birds of a Feather

Extraordinary Chickens by Stephen Green-Armytage

The American Poultry Association website: www. amerpoultryassn.com

Oh Snap! I'm Making Money . . . Now What? A Creative Entrepreneur's Guide to Managing Taxes and Accounting for a Growing Business by Chris Morris, CPA (CreateSpace)

The Vatican Cookbook and *The Lenten Cookbook* by David Geisser (Sophia Institute Press)

The U.S. Small Business Administration: www.sba.gov

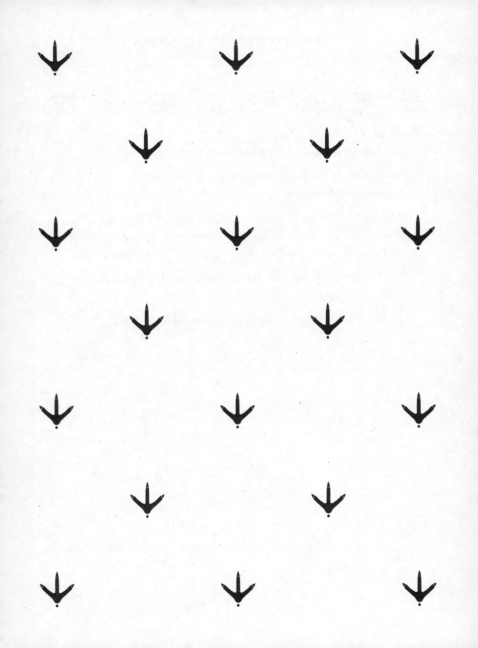

CHAPTER TWELVE

LIVING WELL WITH CHICKENS

THE CHICKENS

Numbers are on the rise for people raising backyard chickens. According to The Happy Chicken Coop website, the Amazon search volume at the beginning of 2020 for baby chick supplies was up 758 percent from the previous year, with searches for chicken nesting boxes up 126 percent. A study done in 2013 by the USDA predicted that by 2019, 5 percent of Americans, or 13 million people, would raise backyard flocks.

In another accounting, about 8 percent of US households had chickens in 2018, according to the American Pet Producers Association. That's about 10 million households enjoying fresh eggs, watching the birds' antics, and avoiding chicken poop.

Reasons for the recent rapid rise are many. Part of it is the COVID-19 pandemic and folks looking to become more self-sufficient, teach responsibility, and enjoy a useful hobby, but also there is interest in knowing where food supply comes from, reducing the possibility of food scarcity, reducing environmental impact, and avoiding consuming meat from factory chicken mills.

The website AGDaily said this:

> Months-long stay-at-home orders connected to the global COVID-19 pandemic contributed to a resurgence of raising backyard chickens in the United States and other countries around the world. People of many walks of life were looking for ways to stay busy while thinking more deeply about where their food comes from and wondering about food scarcity. Because of these trends, evidence points to chickens surging in popularity among landowners.

> *"IT MAY BE THE COCK THAT CROWS, BUT IT IS THE HEN THAT LAYS THE EGG."*
> —MARGARET THATCHER

Heritage Acres Market surveyed nearly three thousand chicken owners about why they keep backyard flocks, details about their flocks, and other interesting tidbits, including the fact that 71 percent of respondents also enjoy gardening and 29 percent have had chickens for less than a year.

While only 10 percent said the pandemic was one of the reasons behind getting chickens, more than 75 percent said it was so they could have fresh eggs. Just over 11 percent said food security concerns were at least part of the reason for creating a backyard flock. Almost 30 percent of flock owners have between one and six birds, and 86 percent of those who responded have named their chickens, according to the survey.

With upward of 10 million people raising chickens, there's a good chance you or someone you know or someone who knows someone has a hen or two or ten wandering around the yard. Folks tell me their stories about favorite chickens, their grandparents' farms, their love of fresh eggs, or their desire to have chickens of their very own.

Chickens, too, are part of our worldwide literary heritage. Books about raising chickens are legion—you've seen many referenced in this book—but there are also children's books, short stories, and novels that feature chickens. The picture book *Chicken in the Kitchen* by Nnedi Okorafor and illustrated by Mehrdokht Amini peaks into the masquerade culture of West Africa; *The Silly Chicken* by Idries Shah, offered in an English-Pashto edition for young readers, is the tale of a chicken who learns to speak as we do, with unintended consequences.

Who hasn't heard of *Chicken Little* and *The Little Red Hen*? *Henrietta, the Early Bird* by the prolific author and illustrator Syd Hoff features a hen eager to make sure everyone is awake on her time schedule. Young children can learn to count thanks to chickens in *Big Fat Hen*, illustrated by Keith Baker.

One of my favorite illustrations from a children's book, which makes me laugh every single time, is from *Animals Should Definitely Not Wear Clothing*, by Judi Barrett with illustrations by Ron Barrett. "Animals should definitely *not* wear clothing," the book begins, mentioning several animals until, "because it might make life hard for a hen."

And there's this upright, stately, and serious hen wearing a pink sleeveless shirt and green-flowered trousers held up by a red belt, with a giant egg stuck out the back of the pants. That egg, stuck in the back end of the green trousers, gets me every time.

Herman Melville, Robert Frost, and P. G. Wodehouse wrote short pieces featuring chickens. The South Korean classic tale *The Hen Who Dreamed She Could Fly* by Sun-mi Hwang teaches all ages about dreams, friendship, and parenthood. Even the esteemed congressman and civil rights activist John Lewis, who died in 2020, has a chicken or two in his past. Jabari Asim and Caldecott Honor-winning illustrator E. B. Lewis offer a fascinating look at his boyhood in *Preaching to the Chickens: The Story of Young John Lewis*.

Chickens continually turn up in amazing places. Sculptor Diane Mason's *Charmin' Charlie* and *Three Hens and a Chick* are on display at the Frederick Meijer Gardens & Sculpture Park. Simone Chickenbone's product line includes 100% Pure Free Range Chicken Poop Lip Junk, which declares on each stick, "Contains no poop." For a look at the full product line, visit www.ilovechickenpoop.com.

The rooster has long been a symbol of Christianity, found pictured in the Roman catacombs, on weathervanes atop old churches across Europe, and in artwork. The rooster is often associated with the disciple Peter, who Jesus predicted would deny knowing him three times before the rooster crowed on the

morning of his crucifixion. As it said in Matthew 26:74–75, "Then he began to call down curses, and he
swore to them, 'I don't know the man!' Immediately a rooster crowed. Then Peter remembered the word Jesus had spoken: 'Before the rooster crows, you will disown me three times.' And he went outside and wept bitterly."

The rooster symbolizes Peter's denial but also his remorse and repentance. There is also a wonderful verse in scripture from the life of Jesus where he laments over the rejection he receives from his people as messiah: "Jerusalem, Jerusalem, you who kill the prophets and stone those sent to you, how often I have longed to gather your children together, as a hen gathers her chicks under her wings, and you were not willing" (Luke 13:34).

Chickens in YA Fiction

For Ellen Airgood, chickens are a key part of her young adult novel *Prairie Evers: A Novel*. Prairie, whose family moved to New York State from North Carolina, must come to terms with her new home without her grammy. She decides that raising chickens

> "I HAVEN'T CHECKED, BUT I HIGHLY SUSPECT THAT CHICKENS EVOLVED FROM AN EGG-LAYING ANCESTOR, WHICH WOULD MEAN THAT THERE WERE, IN FACT, EGGS BEFORE THERE WERE CHICKENS. GENIUS."
> —TA-NEHISI COATES

is just the ticket to help her adjust. Her parents, naturally, ask her why.

"I like the looks of them. They have those funny bodies, all round and fat, and then those skinny little heads up top. I think it'd be fun to have a bunch of them running around," Prairie said, also pushing for a rooster.

She remembers, "Our neighbor lady back home, Mrs. Perkins, had a big white rooster called Otis, and he crowed so loud, it was like he believed he was the one responsible for waking up the sun each day. In fact, he didn't just crow in the morning but whenever the mood struck him all day long."

Airgood said that the same April evening, as heavy rainy slush fell on her Upper Peninsula cabin, that she heard Prairie Evers's voice in her head, she also heard chickens and Prairie telling her the chickens' names. Airgood could see and hear Prairie, recognizing her personality right off. She started writing immediately.

"That's the only time it's ever happened that way; I wish it would happen again," said Airgood, who runs a diner in Grand Marais, Michigan, on the southern shore of Lake Superior. "Others have said it's a gift from the universe and be glad it ever happened. I followed that voice wherever it happened to go."

> **"CREATIVE CONFIDENCE IS ABOUT BELIEVING IN YOUR ABILITY TO CREATE CHANGE IN THE WORLD AROUND YOU."**
> —TOM AND DAVID KELLEY, CREATIVE CONFIDENCE

Airgood's mom grew up on a farm, her father an egg man. Her mom loved the artwork and craftwork associated with chickens but didn't like the actual birds. "I adored my mom and am glad I had the chance to put chickens in the book. She really liked it and was able to read it before she died."

This writer/restauranteur from the way Up North in Michigan holes up, especially in the winter, and writes like mad, as well as writes in the cracks of her life. "I write a lot more in the winter, and in the spring, summer, and fall, I'm mentally hanging out with the characters. And running a restaurant made me far more interested in getting to know people. A life of paying attention to people made me see more characters than I might have otherwise."

Chickens are literally everywhere, and many a creative throughout history has found a way to put these glorious birds somehow, somewhere in their work.

THE CREATIVE

Lisa Steele got her first batch of hens in 2009. She wanted something to keep herself busy while her husband worked in IT for the US Navy. Plus, she realized that her original plan to be an accountant wasn't right for her. She started posting about her backyard chickens on Facebook, drawing more and more followers who asked her the same questions over and over.

She started blogging in January 2012 so she could provide a link to readers who kept asking the same questions. Lisa thought she'd write twenty posts, answer all the questions, and be done.

Wrong. She now has about six hundred posts and runs a thriving business called Fresh Eggs Daily. There's the website, books, recipes, DIY crafts, gardening advice, and the television show "Welcome to My Farm" that debuted in 2022.

"I take each opportunity as it comes," said Lisa from her farm in Maine. "This whole thing appealed to me because I get bored really easily. I'm doing so many different things: blogging, taking photos, caring for the hens. Every day is something different, and there are so many levels of creativity."

She's made curtains for the coop, built a swinging bench and treat holders, shiplapped the coop, created new nesting boxes, baked breads and treats for the flock, and dabbled in DIY projects like signs for the coop, homemade chicken brooders, and chicken-shaped beanbags.

Lisa's book, *The Fresh Eggs Daily Cookbook*, came out in January 2022 to immediate acclaim. Not only is it full of gorgeous photographs, but the cookbook also offers a history of Fresh Eggs Daily and Lisa's life—from Wall Street to bookstore owner to chicken aficionado—and a primer on eggs as related to freshness, color, packaging, safety, and the details of cooking with them.

The recipes are mind-boggling to this noncook: Swedish egg coffee; scrambled-egg hand pies; toasty baked egg cups; egg yolk ravioli; homemade mayonnaise; homemade marshmallows. Any recipe that uses an egg, egg yolk, or egg white is here.

"Eggs are so neutral. You can do anything with them, and the leftovers can go into a scramble," said Lisa. "I like to play around with cooking with eggs. There are some things that you think should work, like macaroni and cheese and lobster, but it just doesn't. I tried a bagel and lox and capers, but that didn't work with eggs either."

Lisa Steele didn't start with a plan other than raising chickens. She didn't have a big plan when she left her Wall Street job or when she started the bookstore, which she sold when she married a navy man. "If you make a strict five-year plan, you might miss out on opportunities because you have tunnel vision. I'm taking each opportunity as it comes," she said.

Lisa also clucks at those who say that they wish they could raise chickens or live in the country. "But you can! Nothing is stopping you," she said. "So many people do what they hate, stay at a job they don't like. There is no excuse for saying 'I wish this or that.'"

Taking the Next Right Step

Lisa Steele has built for herself and her family a sustainable life that brings her joy, fresh eggs, an income, and creative challenges. While she is open to new things, she still treats her chickens as the business they are. She meets her needs now with an eye to the future, which brings up the question of sustainability.

Sustainability is part of the chicken equation. Sustainability says we can meet our current needs without compromising our ability to do so in the future. In a wildly simplified scenario, small flocks can provide us eggs (and meat) that we know didn't come from huge chicken farms. Those huge operations can damage the environment and have questionable animal welfare practices, not to mention provide meat pumped full of growth hormones and antibiotics to the public. Small flocks, on the other hand, can provide fertilizer for our gardens, organic food for our tables, and bring joy to our lives. Sounds like a good sustainable equation to me.

For a scientific, detailed look at the chicken business that includes a deep dive into CAFO (concentrated animal feed operation) practices around the broiler chickens we love to eat, read *Chicken: A History from Farmyard to Factory* by Paul R. Josephson.

"Over 53 billion broiler chickens are killed annually for their meat. The broiler's life is short and under the total control of its industrial handlers," he said in the introduction (p. 3). "The broiler is a prisoner in a technological panopticon with no prospects of hunting, pecking and roosting as chickens normally hunt, peck and roost."

Makes one think, doesn't it? Where, exactly, did that rotisserie chicken come from that I got for dinner because I was rushed and didn't have anything in the house and the thought of making dinner was just too much? What am I putting into my body besides the meat? Will my future grandchildren be immune to antibiotics because of how much is in our food already? Will growth hormones cause them damage in some way?

This isn't the place for a dissertation on how chickens became an industrial commodity, and I've been known for enjoying a rotisserie chicken from my grocery store, or at least I did until I realized how much salt is added, but the issue of sustainability and food origin is worth thinking about. So is the matter of food scarcity.

The pandemic forced many of us to think about our ability to secure good, healthy, affordable food as grocery store shelves weren't as full and some comestibles were hard to come by. Backyard chickens could stand in that gap for urban and rural families. I've profiled several nonprofits in my city that raise chickens as well as run community-supported agriculture (CSA) farms, a combination that inserts much-needed fresh and healthy food into the economy of a neighborhood and a city.

Chickens can do their part when it comes to personal and wider sustainability, helping end food scarcity and insecurity, and making life easier and more enjoyable for all. The creative part comes as we work together to build a sustainable community and as we work individually to build a sustainable life.

The Final Cluck

Building a creative life goes way beyond simply deciding to create. The building material for that creative life includes curiosity, courage, planning, protecting your space, surrounding yourself with wise and healthy companions, thinking ahead, and taking the next right steps.

Our family took that next right step when a boy called his mama and we invited one injured hen into our family. We kept taking the next steps with more chicks, better living space, and letting our hens live their best lives in our large yard. It wasn't always easy. There were dark days when we lost a hen. We've cleaned up a lot of poop and mucked out a coop every now and again.

Your dark days of doubt, redirection, rejection, and struggle will come. Yet if you've created a life that feeds you now and prepares you for the future, you can weather the darkness until the sun rises and the rooster crows once again.

These adorable, exasperating, gentle, egg-laying miracles provide more than fresh food. They bring life to those who care for them and benefit from their eggs and meat. They bring joy to all who really see them for the creative, curious, courageous creatures they are. And they open our hearts to love—for one another and for the marvelous genius of the creator, who saw fit to provide a picture of perfection in one small egg.

CLUCKS FROM THE LEFT-BRAIN CHICKEN

When I want to eat a worm, I go find one. When I want a dog food snack, I walk through the open door to steal it. If it's time to lay an egg, I just do it. I don't second-guess or hesitate to do what brings me joy. My final bit of wisdom for you is this: eat the dog food. If you want something, go after it. If painting brings you joy, do it. If you want chickens, get them.

1. Celebrate chickens in your creative medium as you think on the lessons learned in this book.

2. Think about some of the dark days of your creative life. Now remember how the light appeared. Write a paragraph about that experience in that journal you started when you opened this book.

3. What are some of the things, like chickens, that you are passionate about? No matter how humble a subject, you can turn it into joyful creative expression. Remember, some of our literary heroes were not above writing about the commonplace chicken. Get busy on that project!

BROODY THOUGHTS

- If you could have your dream job, what would it be? What's stopping you from pursuing that job?

- What do you need to research/build/acquire to have a backyard flock?

- Where do you stand on issues such as CAFO, sustainability, and food scarcity? What more do you need to learn about these topics?

- Think about the image of a hen gathering her chicks under her wings. What does safety feel like for you in your creative life? Do you have safe place to rest?

- How can you inject more joy into your creativity, creative work, and creative life?

THE STORYTELLING CHICKEN "SUCCESSOR": A SUFI TEACHING STORY RETOLD

Sufism is a form of Islamic mysticism or asceticism, with Sufi teachings including a variety of animals. Let me tell you this tale about one lucky chicken: There was once a mystical master who was nearing the end of his life and looking for his successor to continue his work of helping his community grow in wisdom, compassion, and love. The community all had opinions on who should be his successor, but the wise man already knew. To help his community think more deeply about their priorities, he devised a test. They gathered around him, and he said, "Your task is to go to the chicken coop, choose a hen, then go wherever you like to slay the hen, then bring the slain hen back here for further instructions. My only requirement is that no one sees where, how, or when you sacrifice your hen."

The group set out eagerly, carefully selecting their hens and then heading out and trying to make sure no one, either one of their own or a stranger, would discover the details of their individual sacrifice. One by

(*Continued*)

one, they returned with their sacrificed hens. The spiritual leader nodded and smiled at each one.

Finally, all had returned except one. When she arrived with her chicken still alive, the master spoke sternly: "I thought my instructions were clear. What didn't you understand? Why have you failed at your task?"

The woman began to cry and said, "Master, I tried to do as you commanded, but I could find no place where God would not witness the method, place, or time of the sacrifice of the hen, so I returned to you."

The master's face broke into a radiant smile. "My daughter," he said, "you have done well, and you alone have done the right thing. Your actions and understanding show why you will be my spiritual successor. Now, let us roast these chickens and prepare a feast to mark the occasion for our neighbors and strangers."

The lone surviving chicken seemed to smile in relief, but since chicken beaks are notoriously hard to read, it's not for sure that she actually smiled.

Retold from a version by Anab Whitehouse, *Sufi Teaching Stories* (Brewer, ME: Bilquees Press, 2018).

Birds of a Feather

Lisa Steele's Fresh Eggs Daily website and blog: www.fresheggsdaily.com, *The Fresh Eggs Daily Cookbook* (Harper Horizon) and *Fresh Eggs Daily: Raising Happy, Healthy Chickens . . . Naturally* (St. Lynn's Press)

Creative Confidence: Unleashing the Creative Potential Within Us All by Tom Kelley and David Kelley (HarperCollins)

Chicken: A History from Farmyard to Factory by Paul R. Josephson (Polity Press)

For more information on Ellen Airgood and her YA and adult fiction, visit https://www.ellenairgood.com

Acknowledgments

What started as chicken pictures on Instagram has turned into a book, and for that I thank Broadleaf editor Lil Copan. We've known each other a long time, so when she messaged me on Insta, I paid attention: "So, I'm wondering about a Writing with Chickens book. I'm serious. Want to chat about a book idea?" Thank you, Lil, and the whole Broadleaf family for the efforts you've put into this book.

Thanks also to my beloved writing group, the Guild, who encourage and love me without bounds, but who also aren't afraid to tell me to get off my vent and get started on the chicken book. Thank you Tracy, Alison, Lorilee, and Sharron. In the early stages of this book, thanks to Cynthia for her enthusiasm and encouragement.

Thanks also to the Breathe community. Though the conference doesn't exist anymore, all of you—attendees, speakers, and the Breathe planning committee—fed into my life repeatedly and well.

And to my family, who all exhibit strength in their own spheres and are a constant source of joy:

Bree, whose creative sabbatical models what it takes to build a creative life while balancing the business side of things. She's the perfect Left-Brain Chicken.

Abby, whose toughness in fighting and living with her disease gives me the fortitude to fight my own daily battles.

Jay and Jared, who both work difficult and patience-bending jobs in adult foster care. You both have huge hearts to care for those who need it most. And Olivia, who takes care of Jared and who cares well for her "children" at work.

Ray, who faces down unruly students hourly and does his very best to teach all of them the basics of biology. And takes good care of the chickens.

Kelsey, who offered sage advice on this book and who lives in her strength day after day as a single mom facing down the worst that life can offer, all while raising her beautiful girls.

About the Author

Ann Byle is a freelance writer who currently writes for *Publishers Weekly*, *Grand Rapids Magazine*, and other publications. She began her career writing book jacket and catalog copy before working as book review editor for the Grand Rapids Press. From there she wrote marketing copy for Our Daily Bread Ministries before beginning her freelance career in 1997.

She has cowritten books, including (with Bethany Hamilton) *Soul Surfer Devotions*, *The Edge of Redemption* with Troy Evans, and *When Angels Fight* with Leslie King.

Ann is author of her own books as well, including *The Baker Book House Story*, *Christian Publishing 101*, and *The Revell Story*. With three other freelance writers, she has written *The Joy of Working at Home: Embracing the Freedom, Avoiding the Pitfalls* (an e-book).

Ann lives in Grand Rapids, Michigan, with her husband, Ray, a high school science teacher, and their husky/hound brown/blue-eyed dog/hellion, one crabby cat, and four chickens. Their four young adult children are in and out regularly. She loves to read, knit, thrift, and puzzle. Visit her at www.annbylewriter.com.